BRANCH LINES TO SOUTHEND AND SOUTHMINSTER

Vic Mitchell

MP Middleton Press

Front cover: Battlesbridge is the first station on the Southminster branch and is the scene for this atmospheric impression of a 4-4-2T "Tilbury Tank" in the 1950s, departing west. (W.A.Camwell/SLS coll.)

Back cover top: Rayleigh is the setting for this record of no. 312721 on 7th November 1988 in Network SouthEast colours. The class 312 EMUs were just used in peak hours in their later years. (Colour-Rail)

Back cover lower: No. 307128 waits at Wickford in 1983, with a DMU for Southminster in the bay platform. (Colour-Rail)

Published May 2010

ISBN 978 1 906008 76 5

Design Deborah Esher

Published by
Middleton Press
Easebourne Lane
Midhurst
West Sussex
GU29 9AZ
Tel: 01730 813169
Fax: 01730 812601
Email: info@middletonpress.co.uk
www.middletonpress.co.uk

Printed in the United Kingdom by Henry Ling Limited, at the Dorset Press, Dorchester, DT1 1HD

CONTENTS

INDEX

ACKNOWLEDGEMENTS

We are very grateful for the assistance received from many of those mentioned in the credits also to A.R.Carder, G.Croughton, N.Honeyman, F.Hornby, J.A.J.Jolly, N.Langridge, B.Lewis, C.Phillips, D.T.Rowe, Mr D. and Dr S.Salter and in particular Barbara Mitchell, who checks everything.

I. Route diagram in 1922. (Railway Magazine)

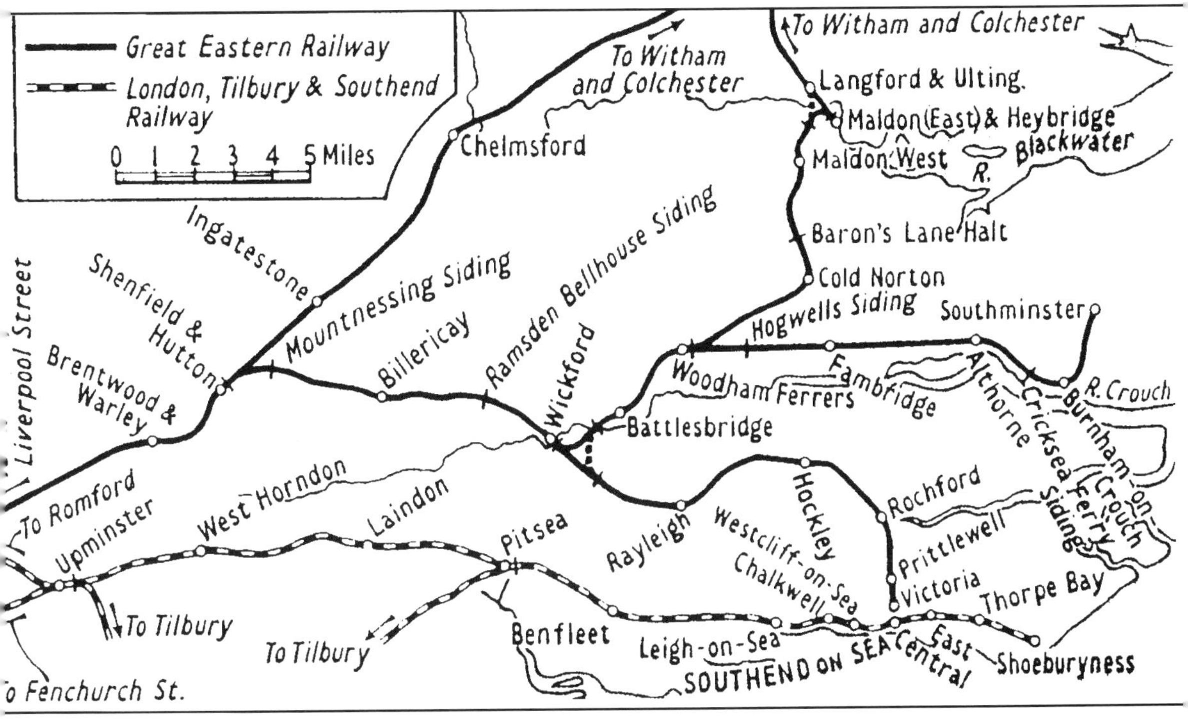

GEOGRAPHICAL SETTING

The Southend line is on the area between the Thames Estuary and the River Crouch, while the Southminster branch is between the latter and the River Blackwater. Maldon is at the Blackwater's first crossing point and was an important commercial centre long before the railways came. It is situated at the confluence of that watercourse with the River Chelmer.

The routes were built entirely in Essex on predominantly London clay. However, overlaying this are significant areas of gravel, notably in the Rayleigh district and near Southminster. The latter deposits have given rise to much rail traffic.

Southminster is described as a once busy place of markets on the Dengie Peninsular, but now a quiet village on a backwater. Burnham-on-Crouch was earlier a busy fishing village (noted for oysters), but is now more concerned with pleasure boating.

The maps are to the scale of 25ins to 1 mile, with north at the top, unless otherwise indicated.

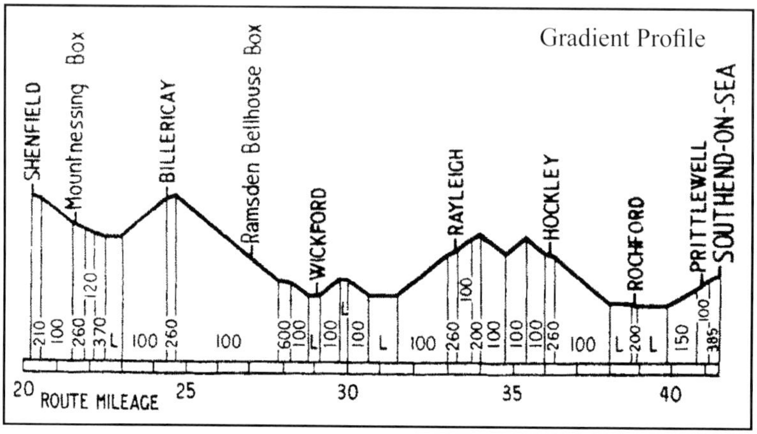

HISTORICAL BACKGROUND

The first line in the area was that of the Eastern Counties Railway, its route opening between Brentwood and Colchester in 1843. It became part of the Great Eastern Railway in 1862. A branch reached Maldon from Witham in 1848.

Southend received a direct line from London in 1856; it was a joint operation by the ECR and the London & Blackwall Railway. It became the main line of the London Tilbury & Southend Railway in 1862 and was extended to Shoeburyness in 1884.

An Act of 16th July 1883 empowered the GER to build a line from Shenfield to Southend, with a branch from it at Wickford to Southminster, plus a further branch from this from Woodham Ferrers to Maldon.

The Shenfield to Wickford section opened to goods on 19th November 1888 and to passengers on 1st January 1889. The corresponding dates for the Southminster route were 1st June 1889 and 1st October 1889. The line between Wickford and Southend opened fully on the latter date, as did the route from Woodham Ferrers to Maldon East.

The GER became part of the London & North Eastern Railway in 1923 and this formed most of the Eastern Region of British Railways upon nationalisation in 1948.

The Woodham Ferrers - Maldon East section lost its passenger service from 11th September 1939. Freight continued until 1st April 1953; other withdrawals are noted in the captions.

Electric services at 1500 volts DC began between Shenfield and Southend Victoria on 31st December 1956. The change to 6250 volts AC took place in November 1960 and it was increased to 25kV on 25th January 1979. The final steam workings were in 1961. Electrification of the Southminster branch followed on 12th May 1986 and the lines became part of Network SouthEast on 10th June of the same year.

Privatisation resulted in the routes being branded First Great Eastern on 5th January 1997 when FirstBus was awarded a 7¼ year franchise. This became First Group, but the operation was transferred to National Express, which applied the meaningless name of 'one' from 1st April 2004. It was rebranded National Express East Anglia in 2008.

PASSENGER SERVICES

The first timetable showed weekday departures east from Shenfield to Wickford at 8.10, 9.45am and 3.45, 5.4, 8.9pm, with a 1.22pm to Billericay only. There was an extra one on Wednesdays and two on Fridays, but none on Sundays.

In the following year, Southend received seven trains on weekdays, two extra on Saturdays and only two on Sundays. One of the Saturday trains ran to Colchester and used long lost curves at the junctions near Maldon and Wickford. Southminster received five on weekdays only and Maldon likewise.

The Colchester-Southend service lasted until 1895. By 1909, Southend had 16 arrivals, with 4 on Sundays. The figures for Southminster were 9 and 2, while Maldon had 5 and 0. The latter had trains on Sundays from 1924 until 1931.

Restaurant car trains to Southend were introduced in 1911, with a journey time of 65 minutes for the 5.27pm departure from Liverpool Street. The one leaving at midnight only required one hour exactly. Restaurant cars were withdrawn in January 1917, but a Pullman car was included on one business train between November 1920 and the Spring of 1924.

In 1938, Southend received 48 trains (41 on Sundays), while Southminster had just 9 (6 on Sundays). Maldon trains were in their final complete year and there were six, weekdays only.

World War II brought severe cuts to 28 (12) to Southend and 9 (2) to Southminster. By 1956, the former were 33 (16) and the latter 11 (2). The introduction of electric services on the main route and DMUs on the branch brought vast improvements. The figures would be tedious to itemise in detail, but the basic frequency has been three per hour to Southend and hourly to Southminster. The Sunday service to the latter has been variable, with cessation in January 1969, Summer only in 1973-74 and restoration in May 1979.

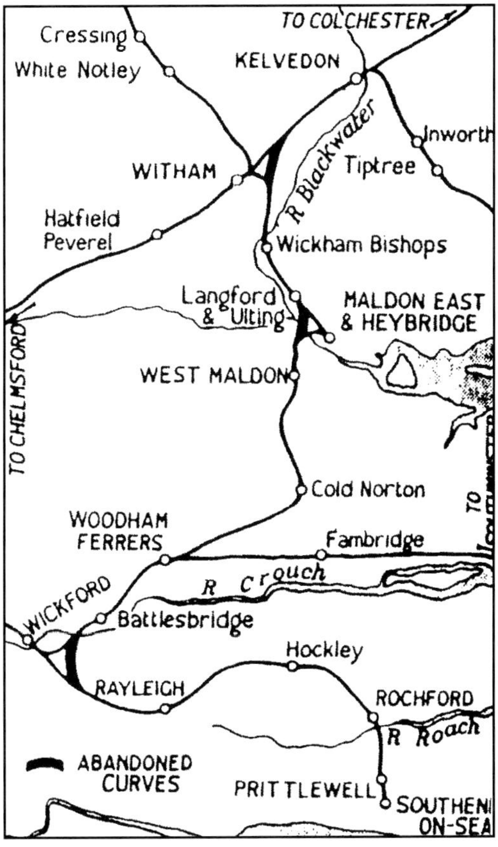

II. The diagram features the connections which were used by a Colchester-Southend service. It allowed about 4½ hours in Colchester on Saturdays, which was market day.

SHENFIELD, WICKFORD, MALDON, SOUTHMINSTER, and SOUTHEND-ON-SEA.—Great Eastern.

Down.	mrn	mrn	mrn	aft	aft	aft	aft	aft	aft	aft	Sndys	Sndys
Liverpool Street, LONDON 132 ....dep	7 8	9 3		12 5	2 3	2 45	4 25	....	5 35	7 10	1018	6 40
COLCHESTER 137 ... "	6 47	8 33		1050	....	2 25	....	4 25	4b12	6 57	1010	6 16
Shenfield and Hutton dep	8 15	9 47		1250	2 50	3 41	5 6		6 12	8 10	1130	7 43
Billericay	8 23	9 55		1258	2 58	3 48	5 14		6 20	8 18	1138	7 51
Wickford ....arr	8 31	10 3		1 6	3 6		5 22		6 27	8 26	1146	7 59
Wickford ....dep	8 36	10 8		1 11		Stop	5 27		....	8 31	....	....
Battlesbridge	8 44	1015	11 7	1 18			5 34		....	8 38	....	....
Woodham Ferris ....arr	8 50	1021	1113	1 24			5 40		....	8 44	....	....
Woodham Ferris ..dep	9 3	1025	1114	1 28			5 44		....	8 48	....	....
Cold Norton	9 12	1034	1123	1 37			5 53		....	8 57	....	....
Maldon (West)	9 22	1046	1133	1 47			6 3		....	9 7	....	....
" (East) 135..arr	9 25	1049		1 50			6 6		....	9 10	....	....
Woodham Ferris ....dep	9 0	1022		1 25			5 41		....	8 45	....	....
Fambridge	9 15	1030		1 33			5 49		....	8 53	....	....
Althorne	9 25	1038		1 41			5 57		....	9 1	....	....
Burnham-on-Crouch	9 39	1047		1 50			6 6		....	9 10	....	....
Southminster ...... arr	9 45	1052		1 55			6 11		....	9 15	....	....
Wickford ....dep	8 33	10 5		1 7	3 7		5 24		6 28	8 28	1147	8 0
Rayleigh	8 43	1015		1 17	3 17		5 34	5 45	6 38	8 38	1157	8 10
Hockley	8 56	1022		....	3 24	aft	5 41	5 52	....	8 45	12 4	8 17
Rochford	9 4	1030		1 31	3 32	6 25	5 49	5 58	6 52	8 53	1212	8 25
Prittlewell	9 9	1035		1 36	3 37	6 30	5 54	6 3	6 57	8 53	1217	8 30
Southend-on-Sea 150..arr	9 12	1037		1 38	3 39	6 32	5 56	6 5	6 59	9 0	1219	8 32
			Saturdays only. From Southend-on-Sea to Colchester.		Saturdays only.	b Leaves at 4 55 aft. on Saturdays.		Saturdays only. Via Maldon (West).				

Up.	mrn	mrn	mrn	mrn	mrn	aft	aft	aft	aft	aft	aft	Sndys mrn	Sndys aft
Southend-on-Sea ......dep	7 13	8 43	....	1033	1148	1 45	3 25	4 52		6 10	7 5	8 45	6 45
Prittlewell	7 15	8 45	....	1035	1150	1 47	3 27	4 54		6 12	7 7	8 47	6 47
Rochford	7 20	8 50	....	1040	1155	1 52	3 32	4 59		6 17	7 12	8 52	6 52
Hockley	7 26	....	....	1046	12 1	1 58	3 38	5 5		....	7 18	8 58	6 58
Rayleigh	7 33	9 2	....	1053	12 8	2 5	3 45	5 12		....	7 25	9 5	7 5
Wickford ....arr	7 42	9 11	....	....	1217	2 14	3 54	5 21		....	7 34	9 14	7 14
Southminster ......dep	....	8 18	....		1125	....	3 2			....	6 42	....	....
Burnham-on-Crouch	....	8 25	....		1132	....	3 9			....	6 49	....	....
Althorne	....	8 34	....		1141	....	3 18			....	6 58	....	....
Fambridge	....	8 43	....		1150	....	3 27			....	7 7	....	....
Woodham Ferris ....arr	....	8 51	....		1158	....	3 35			....	7 15	....	....
Maldon (East) ....dep	....	8 23	9 45		1130	....	3 7			....	6 47	....	....
" (West)	....	8 28	9 50		1135	....	3 12		5 3	....	6 52	....	....
Cold Norton	....	8 38	10 0		1145	....	3 22		5 13	....	7 2	....	....
Woodham Ferris ..arr	....	8 48	1010		1155	....	3 32		5 23	....	7 12	....	....
Woodham Ferris ....dep	....	8 52			1159	....	3 36		5 24	....	7 16	....	....
Battlesbridge	....	9 0			12 7	....	3 44		5 31	....	7 24	....	....
Wickford ....arr	....	9 7			1214	....	3 51			....	7 31	....	....
Wickford ....dep	7 43	9 13		....	1219	2 15	3 56	5 27		....	7 36	9 16	7 16
Billericay ....[133	7 52	9 22		....	1228	2 24	4 5	5 40		....	7 45	9 25	7 25
Shenfield and Hutton 134.	8 0	9 30		....	1236	2 32	4 13	5 48		....	7 53	9 33	7 33
COLCHESTER 134....arr	9 18	1042		12 6	....	3c50	5 31	....		...	1040	....	....
133 LONDON (Liverpool St.) "	8 58	1010		....	1 27	3 10	5 15	6 44		....	8 55	1040	8 30
			c Saturdays only.	Saturdays only. Via Maldon (West).				Saturdays only.	From Colchester to Southend-on-Sea. Saturdays only.				

February 1890

LONDON, SHENFIELD, WICKFORD, MALDON, SOUTHMINSTER, ROCHFORD, and SOUTHEND-ON-SEA.—Great Eastern.

Week Days.

Miles from Shenfield	Down.	mrn	mrn	1&3	1&3	1&3	1&3	aft	aft	aft	aft	aft	aft
	Liverpool Street..dep	5 12	5 28	6 55	9 1	1044	1210	....	....	1248	....	1 20	1 26
	Stratford (W. H.) "	5 22	5 42	7 6	9 12	1054	1219	....	....	....	....	....	....
	306 COLCHESTER...dep	....	....	....	8 20	9 44	11 1	....		....	....	....	....
—	Shenfield & Huttndep	5 56	6 33	8 0	9 48	1137	1245	1253		....	....	....	....
4¼	Billericay	....	6 42	8 8	9 56	1145	....	1 1		1 24	....	....	2 4
8¼	Wickford ....arr.	....	6 49	8 15	10 3	1151	....	1 8		1 30	....	....	2 10
—	Wickford ....dep	....	6 59	8 23	1010	....	....	1 14		....	....	....	2 11
11¼	Battlesbridge	....	7 5	8 29	1016	....	....	1 20		....	....	....	....
13¼	Woodham Fer....arr.	....	7 10	8 34	1021	....	....	1 25		....	....	....	2 20
—	Woodham Fer.dep.	....	....	8 46	1038	....	....	....	1 35				2 26
17¼	Cold Norton	....	....	8 54	1046	....	....	....	1 43				2 34
21	Maldon (West)	....	....	....	....	....	....	....	....				....
22¼	303 " (East) † arr.	....	....	9 5	1057	....	....	....	1 54				2 45
—	Woodham Fec....dep.	....	7 13	8 41	1024	....	....	1 27	....				2 22
17	Fambridge	....	7 23	8 48	1032	....	....	1 34	....				2 29
20	Althorne	....	7 29	8 54	1038	....	....	1 40	....				2 35
23	Burnhm-on-Crouch.	....	7 36	9 1	1045	....	....	1 48	....				2 41
25¼	Southminster...arr.	....	7 41	9 6	1049	....	....	1 53	....				2 45
—	Wickford ....dep.	....	6 53	8 17	10 6	1153	....	1 11	....	1 31	1 36	....	2 15
12¾	Rayleigh	....	7 2	8 26	1015	12 2	....	1 20	....	....	1 45	....	2 24
15¾	Hockley	....	7 8	8 32	1021	12 8	....	1 26	....	....	1 51	....	2 30
18¼	Rochford	....	7 14	8 38	1027	1214	1 7	1 32	....	....	1 57	2 17	2 36
20¼	Prittlewell ....[626	6 20	7 18	8 42	1031	1218	1 11	1 36	....	1 46	2 1	2 21	2 40
21¼	Southend-on-Sea .arr.	6 23	7 21	8 45	1035	1221	1 14	1 39	....	1 49	2 4	2 25	2 43
									Except Saturdays.	Saturdays only.	Saturdays only.	Saturdays only.	Saturdays only.

Down.	aft	aft	aft	aft	aft	aft	aft	1&3	1&3	1&3	aft	aft	aft	aft	aft	aft	aft	aft
Liverpool Street..dep	1 50	....	1 42	2 30	....	2 40	....	3 0	3 25	4 18			4 48	5 18	5 36	....	....	....
Stratford (W. H.) "	....	....	1 52	....	....	....	....	....	....	....			....	....	....	....	....	....
306 COLCHESTER...dep	....	....	1 22	....	....	1 22	....	1 22	....	....			....	....	4 0	....	....	....
Shenfield & Huttndep	2 22	2 27	2 40	....	....	3 22	....	3 33	4 15	4 58			5 19	....	6 8	....	6 12	6 12
Billericay	....	2 35	2 48	....	....	3 29	....	3 40	4 23	5 6			....	....	....	....	6 20	6 20
Wickford ....arr.	....	2 42	2 53	3 11	....	3 35	....	3 46	4 30	5 13			5 30	....	6 19	....	6 27	6 27
Wickford ....dep	....	....	....	....	....	3 37	3 56	....	....	....	5 19	5 23		....	....	6 23	....	
Battlesbridge	....	....	....	....	....	3 43	4 [illegible]	....	....	....	5 25	5 29		....	....	6 29	....	
Woodham Fer....arr.	....	....	....	....	....	3 48	4 7	....	....	....	5 30	5 34		....	....	6 34	....	
Woodham Fer.dep.									....	....	5 35	5 39			....	6 39		
Cold Norton									....	....	5 44	5 48			....	6 47		
Maldon (West)									....	....	....	....			....	....		
303 " (East) † arr.									....	....	5 55	5 59			....	6 58		
Woodham Fec....dep.						3 50	4 9		....	....	5 32	5 36			....	6 33		
Fambridge						3 57	4 16		....	....	5 39	5 43			....	6 42		
Althorne						4 3	4 22		....	....	5 45	5 49			....	6 49		
Burnhm-on-Crouch.						4 10	4 30		....	....	5 51	5 55			....	6 55		
Southminster...arr.						4 14	4 36		....	....	5 55	5 59			....	7 0		
Wickford ....dep.	....	2 43	2 55	3 12	3 16	....	....	3 48	4 33	5 15	....	....	5 31	....	6 20	....	6 29	6 31
Rayleigh	....	2 52	3 4	....	3 25	....	....	3 57	4 42	5 24	....	....	5 39	....	6 29	....	6 38	6 40
Hockley	....	2 58	3 10	....	3 31	....	....	4 3	4 48	5 30	....	....	....	....	....	....	6 44	6 46
Rochford	....	3 4	3 16	....	3 37	....	....	4 9	4 54	5 36	....	....	....	....	....	....	6 50	6 52
Prittlewell ....[626	2 49	3 8	3 20	3 28	3 41	....	....	4 13	4 58	5 40	....	....	5 48	6 15	6 40	....	....	....
Southend-on-Sea .arr.	2 53	3 11	3 23	3 32	3 44	....	....	4 16	5 1	5 43	....	....	5 51	6 18	6 44	....	6 56	6 58
	Saturdays only.	Saturdays only.	Except Saturdays.	Saturdays only.	Saturdays only.	Sats. only.	Except Sats.	Saturdays only.			Except Saturdays.	Sats. only.	Except Saturdays.	Except Saturdays.		Except Saturdays.	Except Saturdays.	Saturdays only.

Week Days—Continued.

Down.	aft	aft	aft	aft	aft	aft	1&3	1&3	1&3	aft	aft	aft	1&3	1&3	aft	aft	ngt.
Liverpool Street .....dep.	6 5	....	6 26	....	7 10	....	8 2	8 2	8 2	....	8 45	....	9 45	9 45	....	11 0	12 0
Stratford (W. H.) .... "	....	....	....	....	....	....	....	....	....	....	....	....	....	....	....	....	....
306 COLCHESTER ....dep.	5 22	....	5 22	....	....	....	7 11	7 11	7 11	....		....	8 43	8 43	....	....	....
Shenfield and Hutton dep.	6 37	6 41	6 58	7 4	7 43	7 48	8 38	8 40	8 43	....	9 22	....	1019	1019	1023	1148	1233
Billericay		6 48	....	7 12		7 56	....	8 43	8 51	....	9 29	....	....	1026	1031	....	1240
Wickford ....arr.		6 54	....	7 19		8 3	....	8 54	8 58	....	9 35	....	....	1032	1038	....	1246
Wickford ....dep.			....	....		....	....	....	....	9 4	....		....	....	....	....	....
Battlesbridge			....	....		....	....	....	....	9 10	....		....	....	....	....	....
Woodham Ferrers....arr.			....	....		....	....	....	....	9 15	....		....	....	....	....	....
Woodham Ferrers.dep.			....	....				....		....	....					....	....
Cold Norton			....	....				....		....	....					....	....
Maldon (West)			....	....				....		....	....					....	....
303 " (East) † ......arr.			....	....				....		....	....					....	....
Woodham Ferrers....dep.	....		....	....	....			....		9 17	....					....	....
Fambridge	....		....	....	....			....		9 24	....					....	....
Althorne	....		....	....	....			....		9 30	....					....	....
Burnham-on-Crouch	....		....	....	....			....		9 37	....					....	....
Southminster ....arr.	....		....	....	....			....		9 42	....					....	....
Wickford ....dep	....	6 55	....	7 21	....	8 4	....	8 56	9 0	....	9 36	9 40	....	1033	1039	....	1247
Rayleigh	....	7 3	7 16	7 30	8 1	8 13	....	9 5	9 9	....	....	9 49	....	1042	1048	12 4	1255
Hockley	....	7 9	....	7 36	....	8 19	....	9 11	9 15	....		9 55	....	1048	1054	....	1 1
Rochford	....	7 15	....	7 42	....	8 25	....	9 17	9 21	....	....	10 1	....	1054	11 0	....	1 7
Prittlewell ....[626	7 3	7 10	7 27	7 46	8 11	8 29	9 4	9 21	9 25	....	9 51	10 5	1045	1058	11 4	1213	1 11
Southend-on-Sea......arr.	7 7	7 22	7 31	7 49	8 15	8 32	9 7	9 24	9 28	....	9 54	10 8	1049	11 1	11 7	1216	1 14
	Except Saturdays.	Except Saturdays.			Except Saturdays.	Except Saturdays.	Except Saturdays.	Saturdays only.	Except Saturdays.			Runs 4 minutes later on Saturdays.	Except Saturdays.	Saturdays only.	Except Saturdays.		

Sundays.

Down.	1&3	mrn	mrn	aft	aft	aft	aft
Liverpool Street .....dep.	8 20	9 28	1042	2 50	6 15	8 43	1010
Stratford (W. H.) .... "	8 31	9 40	1056	3 2	6 27	....	....
306 COLCHESTER ....dep.	....	....	1019	....	5 52	7 11	....
Shenfield and Hutton dep.	9 15	1036	12 5	4 2	7 40	9 37	1050
Billericay	9 23	1046	1215	4 11	7 50	9 45	1058
Wickford ....arr.	9 30	1053	1222	4 19	7 57	9 52	....
Wickford ....dep.	....	11 2	....	....	8 5	....	....
Battlesbridge	....	11 8	....	....	8 11	....	....
Woodham Ferrers....arr.	....	1113	....	....	8 16	....	....
Woodham Ferrers.dep.	....	....	....	....	....	....	....
Cold Norton	....	....	....	....	....	....	....
Maldon (West)	....	....	....	....	....	....	....
303 " (East) † ......arr.	....	....	....	....	....	....	....
Woodham Ferrers....dep.	....	1114	....	....	8 21	....	....
Fambridge	....	1121	....	....	8 28	....	....
Althorne	....	1127	....	....	8 34	....	....
Burnham-on-Crouch	....	1134	....	....	8 41	....	....
Southminster ....arr.	....	1140	....	....	8 46	....	....
Wickford ....dep	9 32	1057	1225	4 20	8 1	9 53	....
Rayleigh	9 41	11 6	1234	4 29	8 10	10 2	1111
Hockley	9 47	1112	1240	4 35	8 16	10 8	....
Rochford	9 53	1118	1246	4 41	8 22	1014	....
Prittlewell ....[626	9 57	1122	1250	4 45	8 26	1018	1121
Southend-on-Sea......arr.	10 0	1125	1253	4 48	8 29	1021	1124

† Maldon (East) and Heybridge.

July 1917

LONDON, SHENFIELD, WICKFORD, and SOUTHEND-ON-SEA

Week Days

Miles	Down	mn	mn	mn	mn	mn	mn	mn	mrn	mrn		mrn S	mrn	mrn	mrn S	mrn S	mrn	mrn S	non E	aft E	aft S	aft S	aft S	aft E	aft S	aft S	aft E
—	London (LS) dp.	510	538	..	655	747	..	832	8 45	9 1	..	9 27	10 6	1030	1046	1121	10 49	1156	12 0	..	1218	1248	..	1235	1 20	1 13	1 4
18½	Brentwood & W. "	548	627	..	742	830	..	913	9 27	9 43	..	1021	1043	1116	1129	..	11 45	1234	12 35	..	..	..	..	1 16	..	2 1	158
20¼	Shenfield & H. "	555	633	..	755	836	..	919	9 38	9 49	..	1033	1049	1125	1142	..	11X53	1240	12 42	1246	..	1 20	..	1 28	..	2 7	225
24½	Billericay ..... "	6 3	640	..	8 3	844	..	926	9 44	9 57	..	1039	1056	1132	1148	..	11X59	1246	..	1253	1256	1 27	..	1 32	..	213	231
29	Wickford arr	610	646	..	810	850	..	932	9 49	10 3	..	1045	11 2	1138	1153	12 1	12X4	1253	12 54	1259	..	1 33	..	1 37	..	219	236
	Wickford dep	611	648	721	811	852	859	934	9 50	10 5	..	1046	11 3	1139	..	12 2	12X5	1254	12 55	1 2	..	1 34	141	1 38	..	220	237
33	Rayleigh	620	656	727	820	..	9 5	943	9 56	1014	..	1053	..	1147	..	..	12X11	..	..	1 10	1 8	..	148	1 44	2 8	..	243
36	Hockley	626	7 2	733	827	..	911	949	10 2	1021	..	1059	..	1153	..	..	12X17	..	..	1 16	1 14	..	154	1 50	2 15	..	249
38¼	Rochford	632	7 7	737	832	..	915	954	10 6	1027	..	11 3	1117	1158	..	..	12X21	1 7	1 8	1 21	..	..	158	1 54	2 20	234	253
40¼	Prittlewell [674	636	711	741	836	..	919	958	1010	1031	..	11 7	1121	12 2	..	1217	12X25	1 11	1 12	1 25	1 21	1 49	2 2	1 58	2 24	238	257
41¼	Southend B ar	639	714	744	839	912	922	101	1013	1034	..	1110	1124	12 5	..	1220	12X28	1 14	1 15	1 28	1 24	1 52	2 5	2 1	2 27	241	3 0

Down	aft S	aft S	aft E	aft S	aft E	aft S	aft S	aft S	aft E	aft S	aft S	aft E	aft S	aft	aft E	aft S	aft E	aft	aft E	aft S	aft E	aft S	aft E	aft	aft	aft E		aft E	aft S	aft E	aft E
London (LS) dep.	150	..	2 0	..	..	230	..	223	2 30	258	..	250	..	332	415	..	..	418	448	..	..	..	522	5 0	539	6 1	..	6 5	6 8	626	..
Brentwood & W. "	..	..	234	229	..	..	..	3 7	3 12	325	..	341	350	411	..	4 26	..	448	..	457	..	..	..	540	..	..	..	634	647	656	..
Shenfield & H "	222	227	240	240	244	..	..	313	3 18	331	340	356	4 0	422	..	4 48	4 48	459	520	520	524	..	..	556	610	635	..	640	656	7 2	7 7
Billericay	..	234	..	247	250	..	..	320	3 25	339	346	4 2	4 6	428	..	4 54	4 57	5 5	..	526	530	..	..	6 3	617	..	..	646	7 2	7 9	713
Wickford arr.	..	240	..	253	255	3 9	..	326	3 31	..	351	4 7	411	434	454	5 0	5 3	511	..	531	536	..	..	6 8	623	..	..	652	7 7	..	718
Wickford dep.	..	241	..	254	256	310	314	327	3 33	..	352	4 8	412	435	455	5 1	5 4	512	..	532	537	549	..	6 9	625	..	..	653	7 8	..	719
Rayleigh	..	249	..	3 2	3 3	..	321	335	3 41	351	358	414	418	442	..	5 7	5 10	519	..	538	544	557	6 7	616	633	..	..	7 1	714	721	726
Hockley	..	255	..	3 8	3 8	..	327	341	3 47	..	4 4	420	424	448	..	5 13	5 16	525	..	544	550	6 3	..	622	638	..	..	7 7	720	..	731
Rochford	..	3 0	3 1	313	313	..	331	346	3V52	..	4 8	424	428	452	5 8	5 17	5 20	529	..	548	554	6 8	..	627	643	..	..	712	724	..	736
Prittlewell [674	246	3 4	3 5	317	316	325	335	350	3V56	4 2	412	428	432	456	512	5 21	5 24	533	542	552	558	612	618	631	647	657	..	716	728	731	739
Southend B arr.	249	3 7	3 8	320	319	328	338	353	3V59	4 5	415	431	435	459	515	5 24	5 27	536	545	555	6 1	615	621	634	650	7 0	..	719	731	734	742

Week Days—Continued / **Sundays**

Down	aft S	aft E		aft E	aft E	aft S	aft E	aft S	aft E	aft	aft		aft	aft	aft E	aft S	aft S	aft S	aft	aft	ngt	ngt	Sundays mrn		mrn		mrn
London (L.S) dp	626	646	..	7 10	..	713	713	..	753	7S53	848	..	9 5	9 45	..	..	1028	..	11 0	..	12 0	..	..	..	8 27	..	9 27
Brentw'd & W. "	7 4	..	..	..	..	..	..	745	825	8S25	..	..	9 48	1012	..	..	1056	..	1141	..	1232	..	..	..	9 13	..	1013
Shenf'ld & H. "	710	718	..	..	..	752	752	756	832	8N36	921	..	9 57	1019	1023	1023	11 3	11 7	1152	1156	1239	..	..	..	9 19	..	1020
Billericay	718	724	..	..	..	..	8 0	8 3	838	8Z42	928	..	10 3	..	1030	1031	..	1113	..	12 3	1246	..	..	..	9 27	..	1028
Wickford ar.	724	731	..	..	..	..	8 6	8 9	843	8 45	934	..	10 8	..	1036	1038	..	1119	..	12 9	1252	..	..	..	9 34	..	1035
Wickford dp.	726	732	..	..	754	..	8 7	813	844	8 47	935	..	10 9	..	1037	1039	..	1120	..	1210	1253	1258	8 21	..	9 35	..	1037
Rayleigh	734	741	..	7 56	8 2	..	816	822	..	8 54	943	..	1015	..	1045	1048	..	1127	12 7	1217	..	1 6	8 28	..	9 44	..	1046
Hockley	740	746	..	..	8 8	..	822	828	..	9 0	949	..	1021	..	1051	1054	..	1133	..	1223	..	1 12	8 35	..	9 50	..	1052
Rochford	745	751	..	..	813	..	827	834	..	9 4	954	..	1025	..	1056	11 0	..	1137	..	1227	..	1 17	8 40	..	9 55	..	1057
Prittlewell [674	749	755	..	8 6	817	814	831	838	858	9 8	958	..	1029	1041	11 0	11 4	1125	1141	1216	1231	1 8	1 21	8 44	..	9 59	..	11 1
Southend B ar.	752	758	..	8 9	820	817	834	841	9 1	9 11	101	..	1032	1044	11 3	11 7	1128	1144	1219	1234	1 11	1 24	8 47	..	10 2	..	11 4

Sundays—Continued.

Down	mrn	mrn		mrn		aft	aft		aft	aft		aft	aft		aft	aft		aft	aft		aft	aft	aft		aft	aft	
London (L.S) dp	1027	1057	..	1157	..	..	1227	..	1 27	..	..	..	2 27	..	330	..	..	557	657	..	757	9 27	1038	..	..	1057	..
Brentw'd & W. "	1113	1143	..	1243	..	..	1 13	..	2 13	..	..	..	3 13	..	416	..	..	643	743	..	843	1013	1120	..	..	1144	..
Shenf'ld & H. "	1119	1151	..	1249	..	1253	1 19	..	2 19	..	..	230	3 23	..	422	..	..	649	749	..	849	1019	1127	..	1132	1152	..
Billericay	..	1159	..	..	..	1 1	1 27	..	..	..	..	238	3 31	..	430	..	..	657	757	..	857	1027	..	..	1138	1158	..
Wickford ar.	..	12 6	..	..	..	1 8	1 34	..	..	..	..	245	3 38	..	437	..	..	7 4	8 4	..	9 4	1034	..	..	1144	12 3	..
Wickford dp.	..	12 7	..	..	..	1 9	1 35	..	..	..	..	246	3 39	..	438	540	..	7 5	8 5	..	9 5	1035	..	..	1145	12 4	..
Rayleigh	..	1216	..	..	..	1 18	1 44	..	..	..	..	255	3 48	..	447	549	..	714	814	..	914	1044	..	..	1152	1210	..
Hockley	..	1222	..	..	..	1 24	1 50	..	..	..	..	3 1	3 54	..	453	555	..	720	820	..	920	1050	..	..	1158	1216	..
Rochford	1143	1227	..	1 13	..	1 30	1 55	..	2 43	256	..	3 6	3 59	..	458	6 0	..	725	825	..	925	1055	..	..	12 2	1220	..
Prittlewell [676	1147	1231	..	1 17	..	1 34	1 59	..	2 47	3 0	..	310	4 3	..	5 2	6 4	..	729	829	..	929	1059	1149	..	12 6	1224	..
Southend B a.	1150	1234	..	1 20	..	1 37	2 2	..	2 50	3 3	..	313	4 6	..	5 5	6 7	..	732	832	..	932	11 2	1152	..	12 9	1227	..

LONDON, SHENFIELD, WICKFORD, MALDON, and SOUTHMINSTER

Week Days / **Sundays**

Miles	Down	mrn	mn	mrn	mrn S	mrn S	non E	aft S	aft S	aft S	aft E	aft S	aft E	aft S	aft	aft	aft E	aft S	aft S	ngt V	Sundays mrn		aft		
—	London (Liv St) .... dep.	5 10	655	9 1	1121	1156	12 0	1248	1 27	..	230	240	415	418	539	6x46	7 53	8 48	1028	12 0	9 27	..	757	..	..
20¼	Shenfield & Hutton "	5 55	755	9 49	..	1240	1246	1 20	..	..	318	323	..	459	610	7U18	8 36	9 21	11 7	1239	1020	..	849	..	..
24½	Billericay	6 3	8 3	9 57	..	1246	1253	1 27	2 3	..	325	330	..	5 5	617	7U24	8 42	9 28	1113	1246	1028	..	857	..	..
29	Wickford ...... arr.	6 10	810	10 3	12 1	1253	1259	1 33	2 10	..	331	336	454	511	623	7U31	8 47	9 34	1119	1252	1035	..	9 4	..	..
	Wickford ...... dep.	6 37	830	1017	12 5	1259	1 7	1 44	2 11	2 15	4 0	338	459	520	632	7 36	9 1	9 38	1123	1256	1041	..	910	..	..
31¾	Battlesbridge	6 43	836	1023	1211	1 5	1 13	..	..	2 21	4 6	345	5 5	526	638	7 42	9 7	9 44	1129	..	1047	..	916	..	..
34	Woodham Ferrers .. arr.	6 48	841	1028	1216	1 10	1 18	1 52	..	2 26	411	350	510	531	643	7 47	9 12	9 49	1134	1 5	1052	..	921	..	..
—	Woodham Ferrers dep.	..	850	1032	..	..	1 26	..	..	2 30	..	..	514	537	650	..	..	9 53	..	..	..	..	..	..	..
36½	Stow St Mary Halt ..	..	855	1037	..	..	1 31	..	..	2 35	..	..	519	542	655	..	..	9 58	..	..	..	..	..	..	..
37¾	Cold Norton	..	859	1042	..	..	1 35	..	..	2 39	..	..	523	546	659	..	..	10 2	..	..	..	..	..	..	..
39¼	Barons Lane Halt	..	9 3	1045	..	..	1 39	..	..	2 43	..	..	527	550	7 3	..	..	10 6	..	..	..	..	..	..	..
41¼	Maldon (West)	..	9 9	1051	..	..	1 45	..	..	2 49	..	..	533	556	7 9	..	..	1012	..	..	..	..	..	..	..
42¼	" (East) A 880 arr.	..	912	1054	..	..	1 48	..	..	2 52	..	..	536	559	712	..	..	1015	..	..	..	..	..	..	..
—	Woodham Ferrers .. dep.	6 51	847	1029	1217	1 11	1 20	1 53	..	2 27	412	351	511	533	647	7 48	9 13	9 50	1135	1 6	1053	..	922	..	..
37¼	Fambridge	6 59	854	1036	1224	1 18	1 27	1 59	..	2 35	419	359	518	540	654	7 55	9 20	9 57	1142	1 13	11 0	..	929	..	..
40¼	Althorne	7 5	9 0	1042	1230	1 24	1 33	..	..	2 41	425	4 6	524	546	7 0	8 1	9 26	10 3	1148	1 19	11 6	..	935	..	..
43¼	Burnham-on-Crouch	7F18	9 7	1049	1237	1 31	1 40	2 11	2 38	2J54	432	413	531	553	7 6	8 7	9 33	1010	1154	1 26	1113	..	942	..	..
45¼	Southminster ..... arr.	7 23	912	1055	1242	1 36	1 45	2 16	2 43	2 59	437	418	536	558	711	8 12	9 38	1015	1159	1 31	1118	..	947	..	..

A Malden (E.) and Heybridge B Station for Westcliff & Thorpe Bay. E or E Except Sats. F Arr 7 11 mrn.
J Arr 2 47 aft. N 4 mins *earlier* on Sats. S or S Sats only U 8 mins *earlier* Sats. V Weds ngts & Thurs mrns only.
V 7 mins later on Weds X 7 mins later on Sats x Dep. 6 26 aft Sats. Z 3 mins. *earlier* on Sats.

December
1938

6 May 1968 -
4 May 1969

Wickford and Southminster

Second class only

Mondays to Fridays

Miles																								
	LIVERPOOL STREET .. d	05 24	06 24	07 18	..	08 34	..	1004	1204	..	1404	..	1524	..	1618	1714	..	1754	..	1834	1918	2024
	SHENFIELD & HUTTON d	06 01	07 09	07 47	....	09 11	....	1041	1241	....	1441	....	1601	....	1645	1735	....	1816	....	1901	1945	2101
—	WICKFORD .. d	06 43	07 25	08 03	..	09 28	..	1057	1257	..	1457	..	1619	..	1708	1755	..	1835	..	1915	2000	2121
2½	BATTLESBRIDGE d	47	30	07	....	32	....	1101	1301	....	1501	....	24	....	12	1800	....	39	....	20	04	26
5	WOODHAM FERRERS d	52	35	12	..	37	..	06	06	..	06	..	29	..	17	05	..	44	..	25	09	31
8¼	FAMBRIDGE d	07c01	b43	c21	....	42	....	11	11	....	11	....	34	....	22	11	....	49	....	30	14	36
11¼	ALTHORNE d	05	48	25	..	46	..	15	15	..	15	..	39	..	26	16	..	53	..	35	18	41
14¼	BURNHAM-ON-CROUCH d	10	54	30	....	51	....	20	20	....	20	....	45	....	31	22	....	58	....	41	23	47
16½	SOUTHMINSTER .. a	07 14	07 59	08 34	..	09 55	..	1124	1324	..	1524	..	1650	..	1735	1827	..	1902	..	1946	2027	2152

Saturdays

LIVERPOOL STREET .. d	0524	..	0624	..	0804	..	0944	..	1104	..	1224	..	1344	..	1504	..	1624	1744	..	1904	2024	..	2218
SHENFIELD & HUTTON d	0601	....	0709	....	0841	....	1021	....	1141	....	1301	....	1421	....	1541	....	1701	1821	....	1941	2101	....	2245
WICKFORD .. d	0629	..	0742	..	0857	..	1037	..	1157	..	1317	..	1437	..	1557	..	1717	1837	..	1957	2117	..	2308
BATTLESBRIDGE d	33	....	47	....	0901	....	41	....	1201	....	21	....	41	....	1601	....	21	41	....	2001	21	....	12
WOODHAM FERRERS d	38	..	51	..	06	..	46	..	06	..	26	..	46	..	06	..	26	46	..	06	26	..	17
FAMBRIDGE d	43	....	56	....	11	....	51	....	11	....	31	....	51	....	11	....	31	51	....	11	31	....	22
ALTHORNE d	47	..	0801	..	15	..	55	..	15	..	35	..	55	..	15	..	35	55	..	15	35	..	26
BURNHAM-ON-CROUCH d	52	....	06	....	20	....	1100	....	20	....	40	....	1500	....	20	....	40	1900	....	20	40	....	31
SOUTHMINSTER .. a	0656	..	0810	..	0924	..	1104	..	1224	..	1344	..	1504	..	1624	..	1744	1904	..	2024	2144	..	2335

Sundays

	A										
LIVERPOOL STREET .. d	0704	0904	1004	1104	1304	1504	1704	1804	1904	21 18	..
SHENFIELD & HUTTON d	0748	0941	1041	1141	1341	1541	1741	1841	1941	21 45	..
WICKFORD .. d	0801	0959	1104	1201	1401	1601	1801	1906	2003	22 07	..
BATTLESBRIDGE d	05	1003	08	05	05	05	05	10	07	11	....
WOODHAM FERRERS d	10	08	13	10	10	10	10	15	12	16	..
FAMBRIDGE d	15	13	18	15	15	15	15	20	17	21	....
ALTHORNE d	19	17	22	19	19	19	19	24	21	25	..
BURNHAM-ON-CROUCH d	24	20	1127	24	24	24	24	1929	26	30	....
SOUTHMINSTER .. a	0828	1026	..	1228	1428	1628	1828	..	2030	22 34	..

Heavy figures denote through trains
Light figures denote connecting services

No staff are in attendance at Battlesbridge and tickets are issued on the train
At certain times no staff are in attendance at Woodham Ferrers, Fambridge, Althorne, Burnham-on-Crouch and Southminster and tickets are issued on the train

A From Stratford dep 0725. Second class only
b Arr. 3 minutes earlier
c Arr. 4 minutes earlier

1. Shenfield to Southend

SHENFIELD

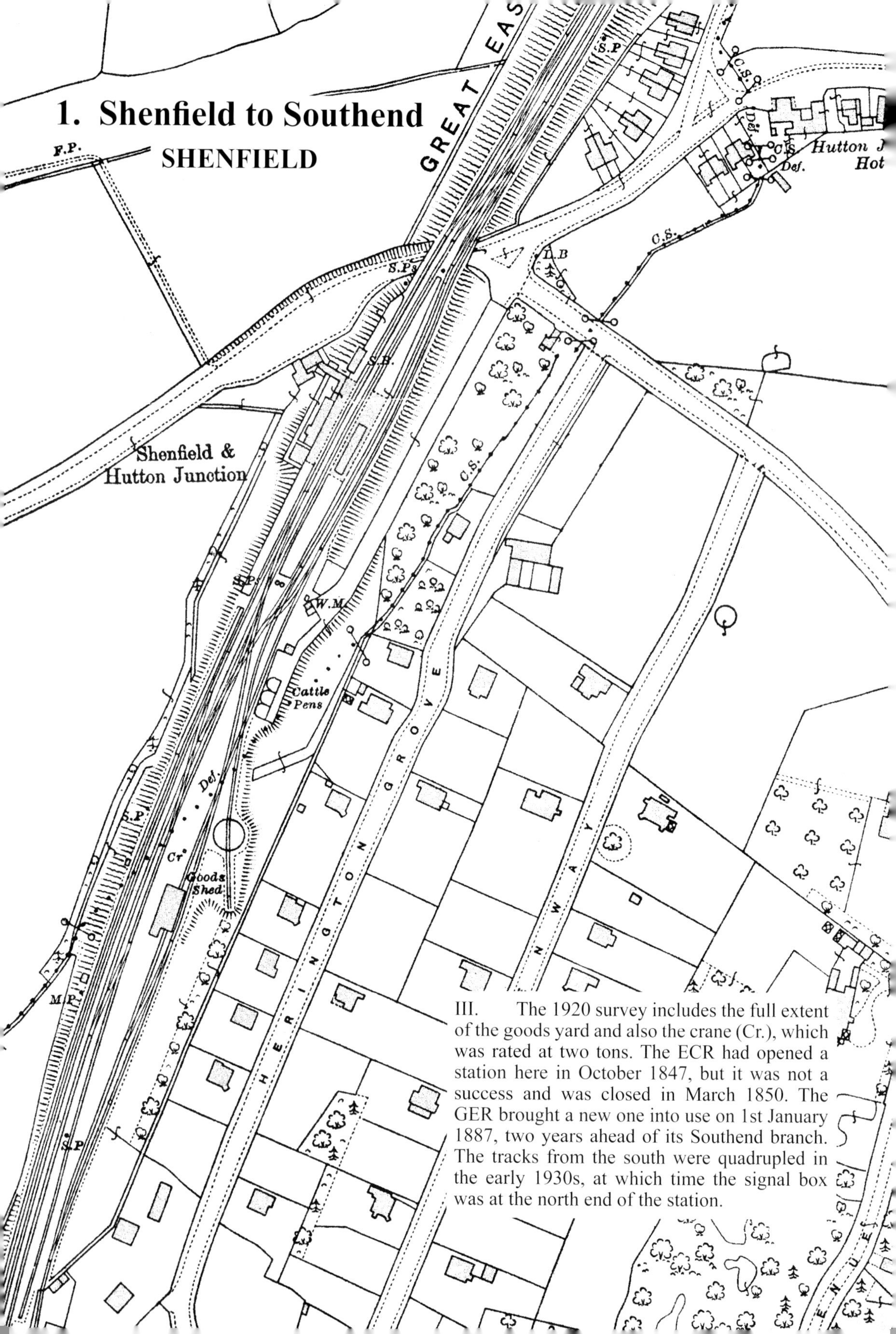

III. The 1920 survey includes the full extent of the goods yard and also the crane (Cr.), which was rated at two tons. The ECR had opened a station here in October 1847, but it was not a success and was closed in March 1850. The GER brought a new one into use on 1st January 1887, two years ahead of its Southend branch. The tracks from the south were quadrupled in the early 1930s, at which time the signal box was at the north end of the station.

1. The north elevation is seen in around 1920, with the house for the station master nearest. The local population was 1692 in 1901 and rose slowly to 5390 by 1961. (P.Laming coll.)

2. A view north in the same era includes all three platforms, with a goods train in the loop. The station was totally rebuilt in 1933-34 and the number of platforms rose to five. (P.Laming coll.)

3. This is the prospective passengers perspective soon after the rebuilding was completed. A wider road and a new bridge over it came at the same time. A new facade arrived in the 1970s. (P.Laming coll.)

4. A southward view in July 1939 features the signal box, which came in 1938 and closed in May 1981. On the left is the goods shed; freight traffic ceased here on 4th May 1964 and a car park followed on its site. (H.C.Casserley)

↓ 5. The suffix "and Hutton" was applied from 1887 until 1969. We see no. E9011 in 1948 still carrying its original number, it becoming 67712 in July 1948. (H.C.Casserley)

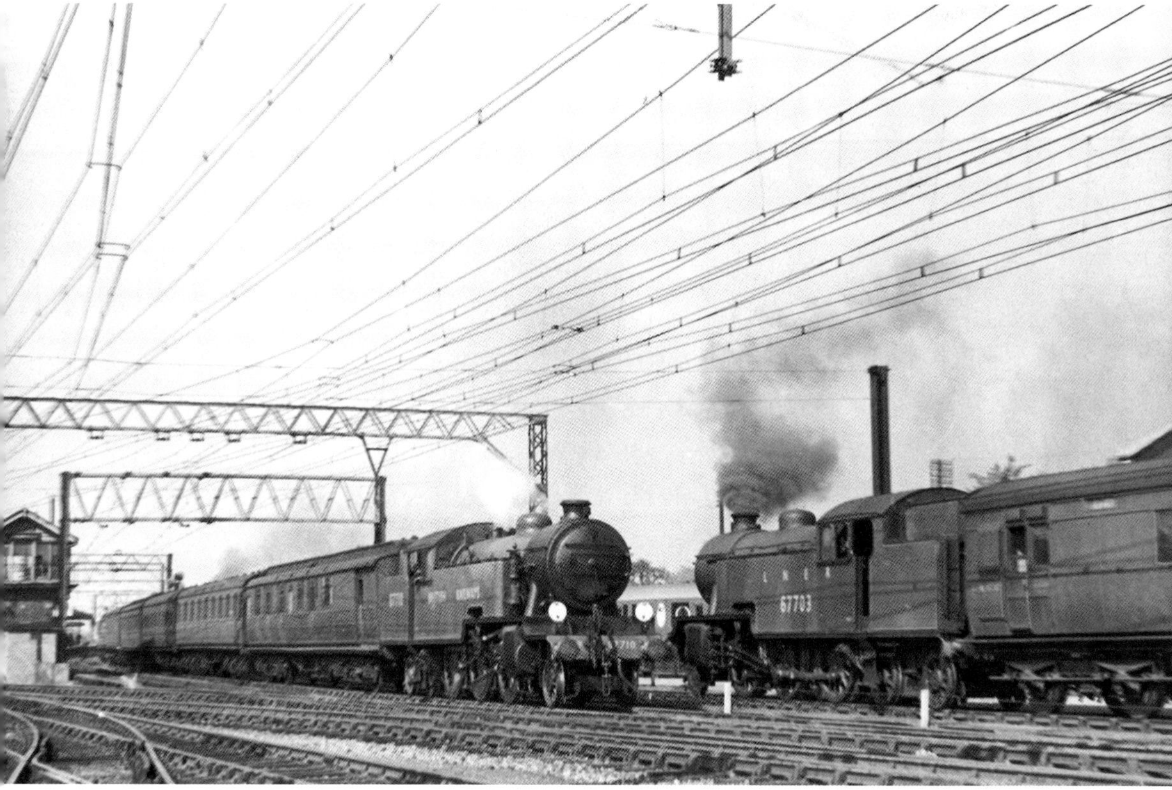

6. Class L1 2-6-4Ts pass, no. 67703 with LNER livery and no. 67710 with BR lettering. The date is 26th June 1948 and electric traction is imminent. (H.C.Casserley)

IV. This diagram shows the limit of electrified tracks in 1949, together with the track arrangement east of the station. The convergence of the Southend lines on the right is at Mountnessing Junction. (Railway Magazine)

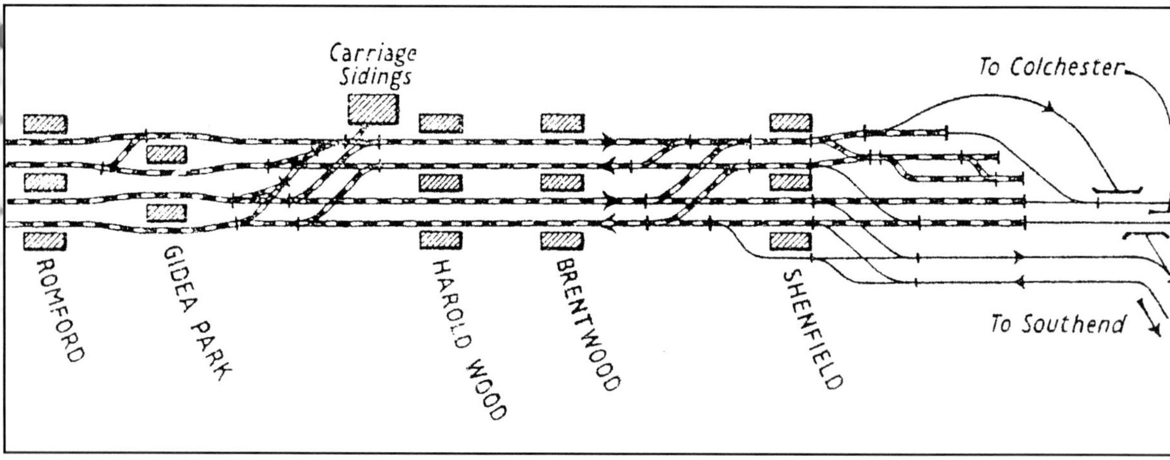

7. Approaching platform 3 is Britannia class 4-6-2 no. 70003 *John Bunyan*, with a down train on 8th April 1961. This class worked to Southend on rare occasions. (R.M.Casserley)

8. We are looking northeast along platform 5, which was termed "down slow". Passing through No. 2 is a D5000 diesel, sometime around 1960. They were built by BR at Crewe in 1959-60 and later classified 24. (Norfolk Rly. Soc.)

9. Our final view northeast is from platform 1/2 and has the Southend lines on the right of centre. The cupboard contained a telephone. (Norfolk Rly. Soc.)

Other views of this station can be found in the *Ilford to Shenfield* album in pictures 102 to 120.

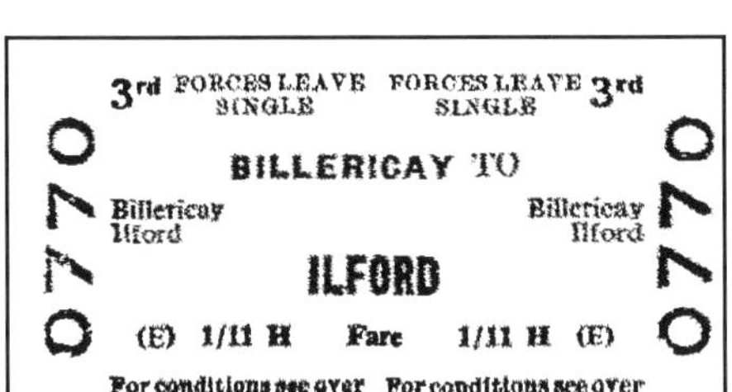

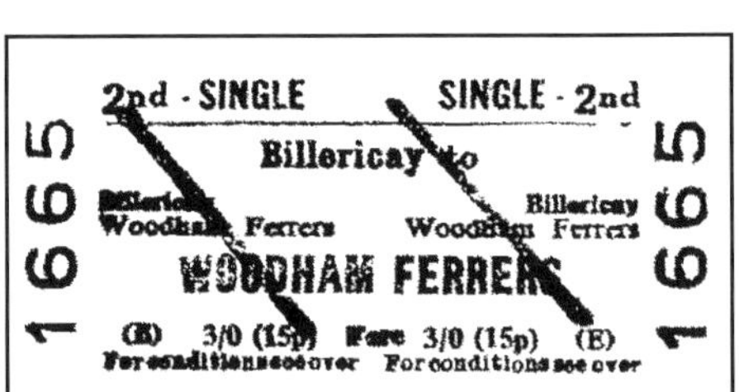

EAST OF SHENFIELD

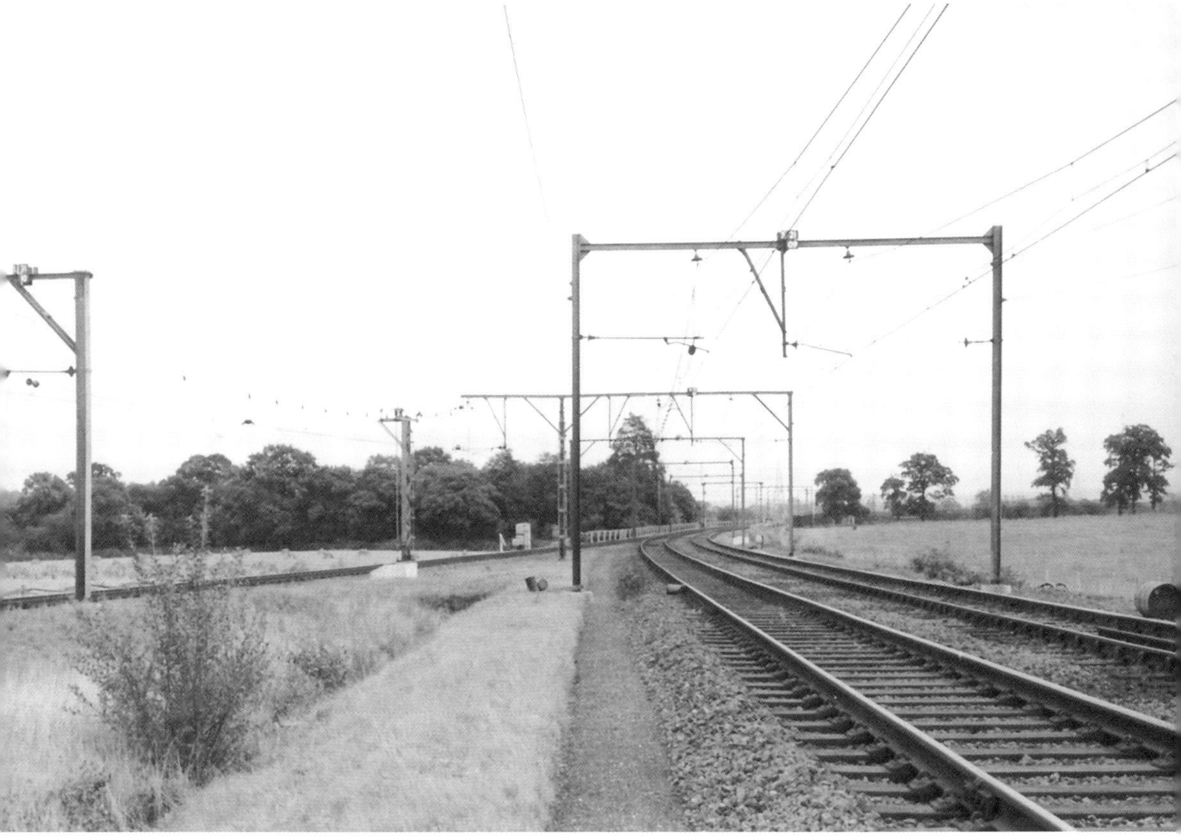

10. Mountnessing Junction is in the background of this view towards Southend. It is where the two down lines converge; the up one is on the right. Mountnessing siding was on the south side and was in public use until 9th August 1965. Its site is now commercial property. (Norfolk Rly. Soc.)

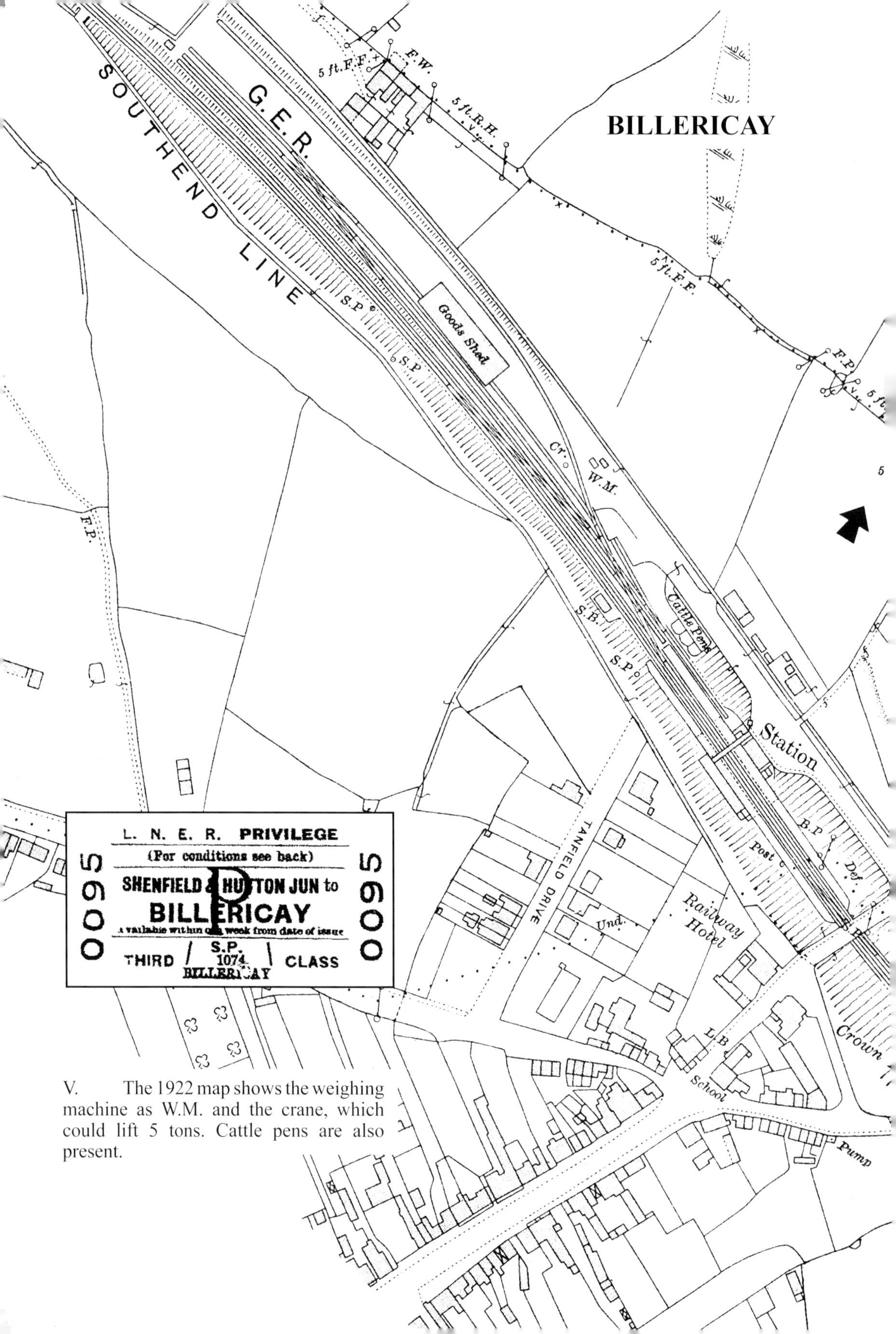

0095

L. N. E. R. PRIVILEGE

(For conditions see back)

SHENFIELD & HUTTON JUN to

BILLERICAY

Available within one week from date of issue

THIRD | S.P. 1074 | CLASS

BILLERICAY

0095

V. The 1922 map shows the weighing machine as W.M. and the crane, which could lift 5 tons. Cattle pens are also present.

11. An early postcard view towards Shenfield has the goods shed in the distance. The entrance and booking office are on the first floor. (P.Laming coll.)

12. Fore-runners of the ubiquitous surveillance camera keep an eye on the photographer from the footbridge and the down platform eastern end, the latter well armed with a defensive broom. A ghostly female figure haunts the area by the canopy supports, whilst milk churns help to date the view. Note the old carriage on the left in this eastward panorama. (P.Laming coll.)

← 13. This is one of the deepest cuttings on the route and is spanned by bridges for Stock Road (nearest) and Norsey Road. Part is painted white to improve contrast with the red signal arm. (P.Laming coll.)

← 14. The multi-arched bridge is the viewpoint on 3rd August 1953 for recording class B17 4-6-0 no. 61609 *Quidenham* departing for Southend. Colour light signals came into use from Shenfield on 27th February 1938 and to Wickford on 22nd May of that year.
(D.T.Rowe)

15. The nearest locomotive is class J15 no. 65370 and it is blowing off on 19th September 1955. Goods traffic ceased here on 15th June 1967 and the spacious shed was soon demolished. There were two sidings at Ramsden Bellhouse, 2¾ miles east of the station.
(B.Pask)

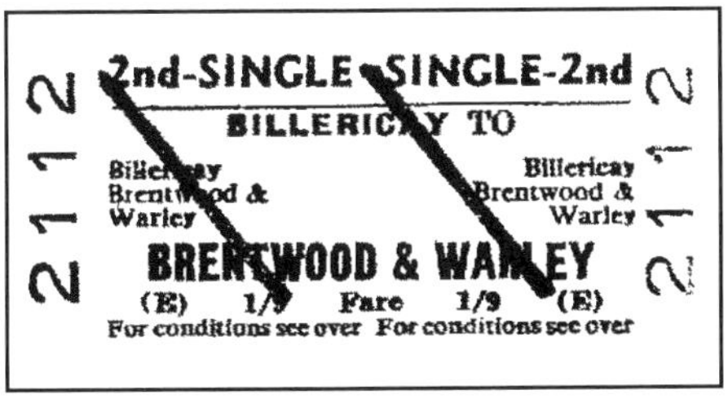

2112
2nd-SINGLE SINGLE-2nd
BILLERICAY TO
Billericay Brentwood & Warley
Billericay Brentwood & Warley
BRENTWOOD & WARLEY
(E) 1/9 Fare 1/9 (E)
For conditions see over For conditions see over
2112

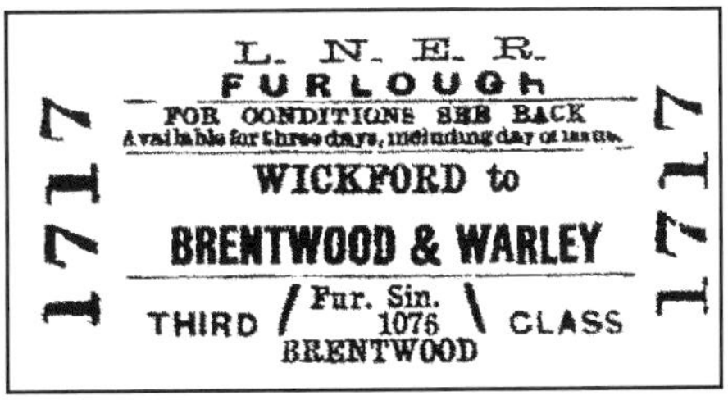

1717
L. N. E. R.
FURLOUGH
FOR CONDITIONS SEE BACK
WICKFORD to
BRENTWOOD & WARLEY
THIRD / Fur. Sin. 1076 \ CLASS
BRENTWOOD
1717

16. An official photograph depicts London-bound passengers on the first day of electric services, 31st December 1956. The seats would no longer blacken light clothing. 16 was the unit number and S indicated that Southend was its depot. (D.Brennand coll.)

17. With pantograph evident, a 4-car class 307 EMU waits to leave for Southend on 5th January 1957 and stands under smoke-stained ironwork. All the station structures were still in place more than 50 years later. There were steps on the cutting wall on the right in 1961 and the trains received yellow ends later. (E.Wilmshurst)

EAST OF BILLERICAY

18. Ramsden Bellhouse was a public goods yard situated on the down side and it is seen on 19th September 1955. It closed on 22nd August 1960, the site having received the first of the transformers for the electrification scheme by rail. (B.Pask)

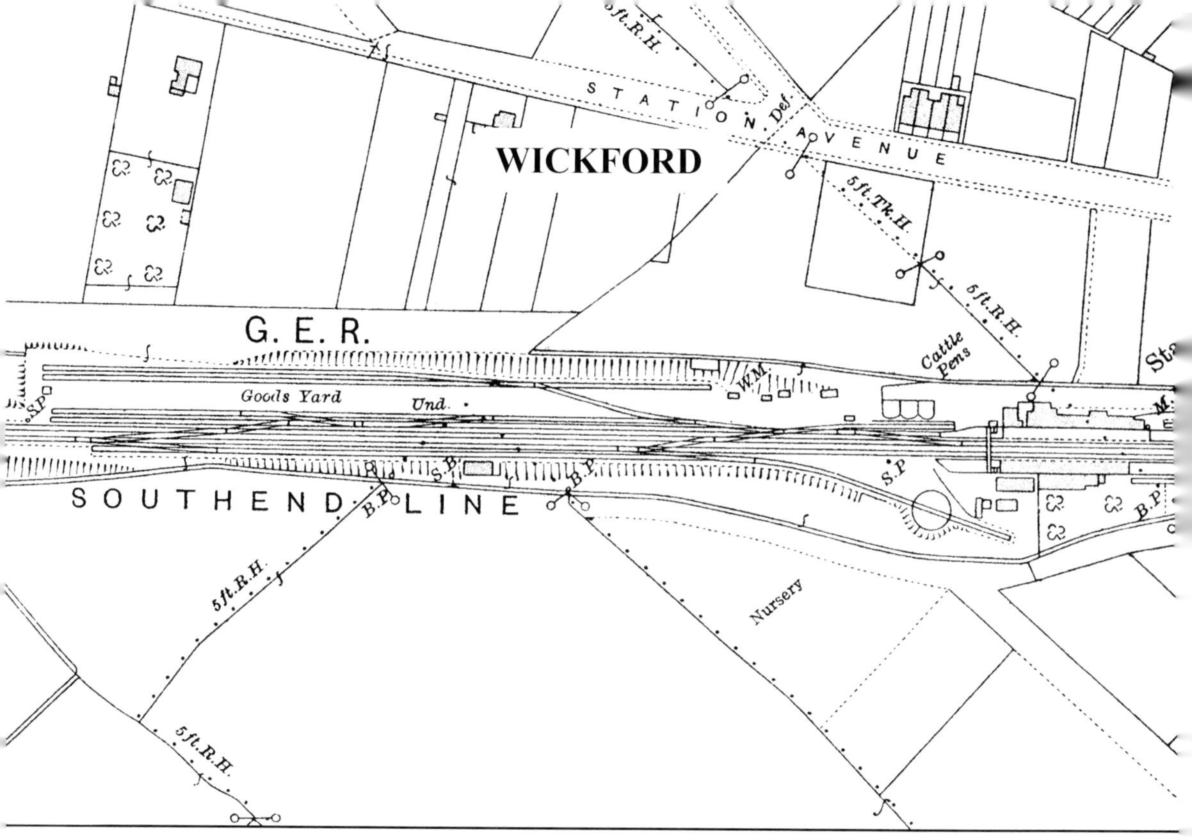

VI. The 1922 edition has the infant River Crouch on the right, together with evidence of use by the GER of its water. Two locomotives were allocated here in January 1922 for branch work: a class T26 2-4-0 and a class Y14 0-6-0. The yard had a 50ft turntable and closed in 1954. Wickford Yard Box had 30 levers and closed in 1938.

19. The north elevation was recorded in an early postcard. The profile remains the same, but the entrance has been moved to the left of the nearest driver. (P.Laming coll.)

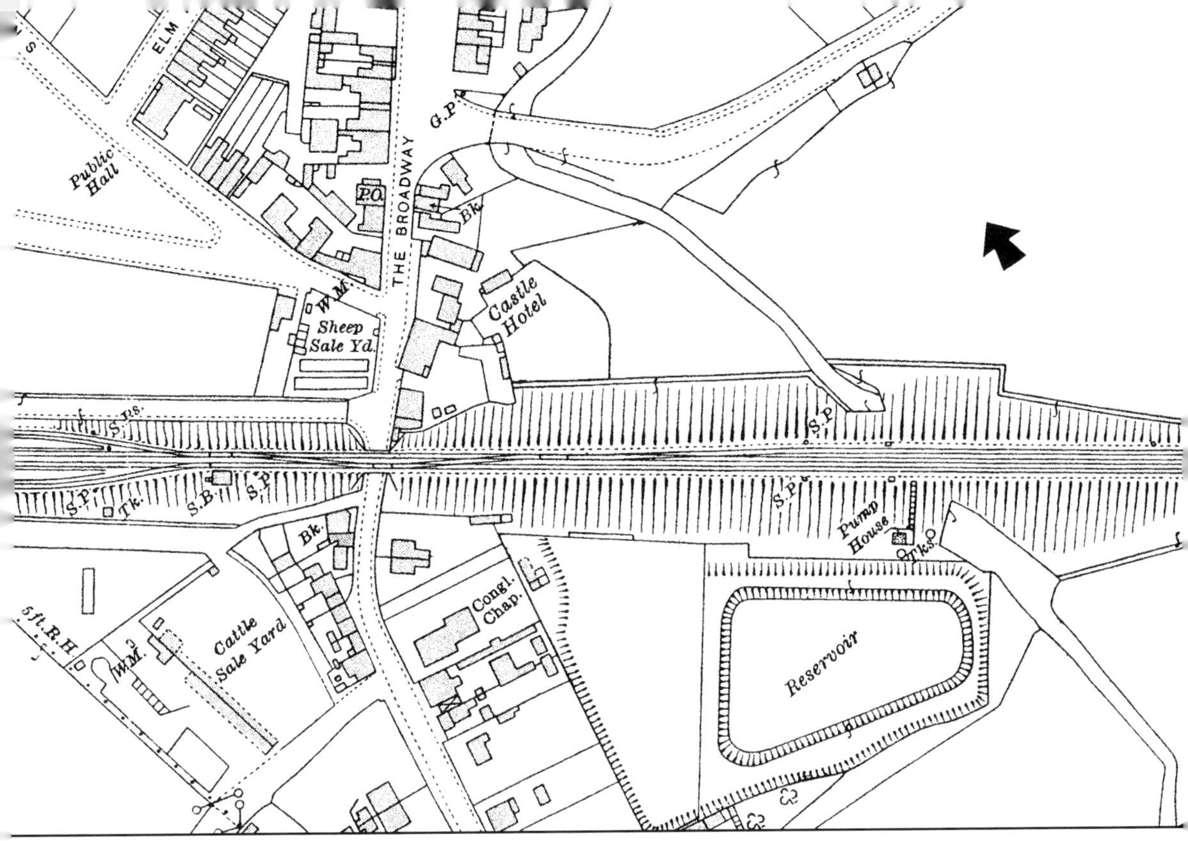

20. The signalman surveys his vast array of signals from his box, whilst another member of staff deals with a further task by the signal for the bay on the right. A train occupies the bay on the left adjacent to a cylinder which probably housed gas. Water columns appear to be only on the country end of the station which suggests that their only user would be the branch train. A land sale notice appears in the field on the right indicating that this country station scene will soon disappear. The locomotive water tank is just in view, next to the signal box. (P.Laming coll.)

21. This view is southeast with the signals for the Southminster branch visible. A train appears to be crossing over to the up line and may well be from that place. The branch signal would seem to indicate that it is destined for the south bay platform. Signals in the distance on the main up line suggest that trains may be directed to any of the three platforms. The down one has a variety of goods on display, including a wooden barrel and rolls and sacks all of unknown content. Wicker baskets may be pigeon traffic, but it is not clear if the birds have flown. At the country end of the station the two white discs are attached to the water columns. (P.Laming coll.)

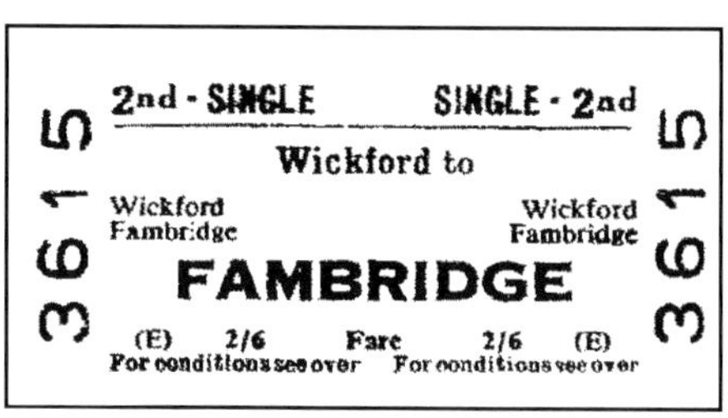

2nd - SINGLE SINGLE - 2nd
3615 3615
Wickford to
Wickford Wickford
Fambridge Fambridge
FAMBRIDGE
(E) 2/6 Fare 2/6 (E)
For conditions see over For conditions see over

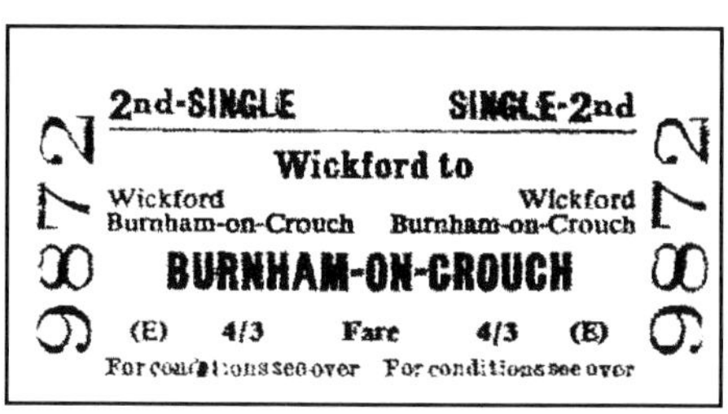

2nd-SINGLE SINGLE-2nd
9872 9872
Wickford to
Wickford Wickford
Burnham-on-Crouch Burnham-on-Crouch
BURNHAM-ON-CROUCH
(E) 4/3 Fare 4/3 (E)
For conditions see over For conditions see over

22. This locomotive appears to be a 0-4-4T of class 61 (1875-1878), no. 244. This class was withdrawn during 1906-1913. The photographer is standing on the downside platform. (P.Laming coll.)

23. This is the London end of the station in June 1938, with class J15 no. 7555 shunting the loco yard siding. On the right is the goods yard, which closed on 5th June 1967. The number of residents rose from 638 in 1901 to 13,787 in 1961. (W.A.Camwell/SLS coll.)

24. Class B12 no. 61576 departs with the 12.10 Shenfield to Southend on 15th March 1955 and will soon pass the junction for Southminster. Trains from that branch would run over the curve on the right and terminate in the up bay. The engine would then propel the empty coaches into a siding in the left distance and leave the guard in it. The locomotive would then proceed to its siding, on the left of picture 23. The guard would later release the train brakes and allow it to run under gravity down the gradient into the down bay. (H.C.Casserley)

25. Evident is one of the DC signals introduced between here and Southend on 26th June 1938. The signal boxes at the intermediate stations were all closed then. Class B12 4-6-0 no. 61561 runs in with the 1.53pm Liverpool Street to Southend service on 10th March 1956. (R.F.Roberts/SLS coll.)

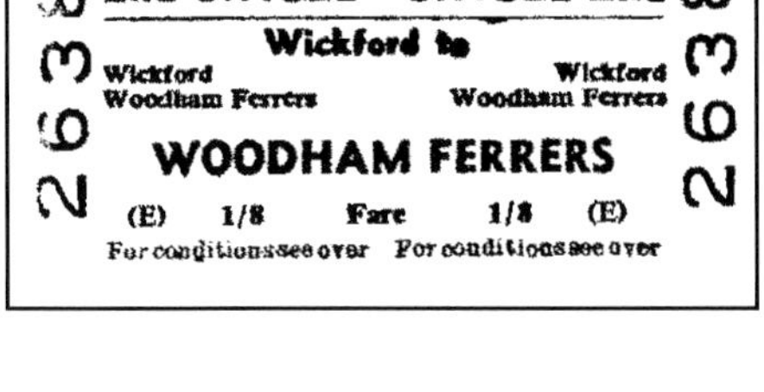
2638 2nd-SINGLE SINGLE-2nd 2638
Wickford to
Wickford Woodham Ferrers | Wickford Woodham Ferrers
WOODHAM FERRERS
(E) 1/8 Fare 1/8 (E)
For conditions see over For conditions see over

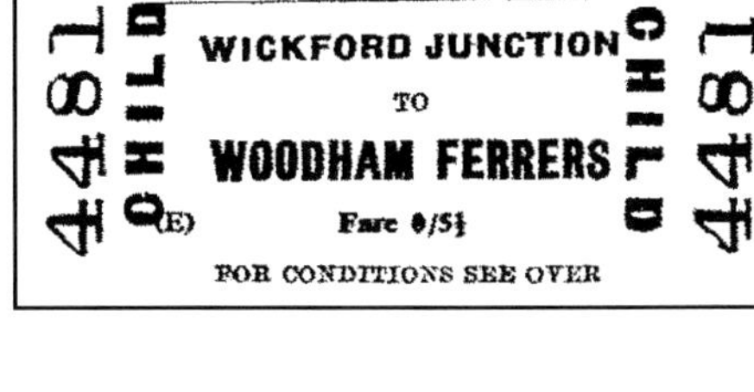
3rd-SINGLE
4481 CHILD
WICKFORD JUNCTION
TO
WOODHAM FERRERS
(E) Fare 0/5½
FOR CONDITIONS SEE OVER
CHILD 4481

26. A DMU stands in the down bay on 25th April 1970 forming the 11.11 to Southminster. Both bays were electrified with the branch in 1986, as were the two sidings at the other end of the station. The up one could take 12 cars and the down one 8, but they were seldom used. (R.F.Roberts/SLS coll.)

27. This is the point of divergence of the branch before its electrification. Wickford signal box controlled the branch to Fambridge. The box had 36 levers and closed on 22nd August 1983, when its work passed to Liverpool Street. It was demolished in 1992, after a new connection was completed. At the north end of the pre-1894 triangular junction was the 22-lever Belchamps Junction signal box. (Norfolk Rly. Soc.)

RAYLEIGH

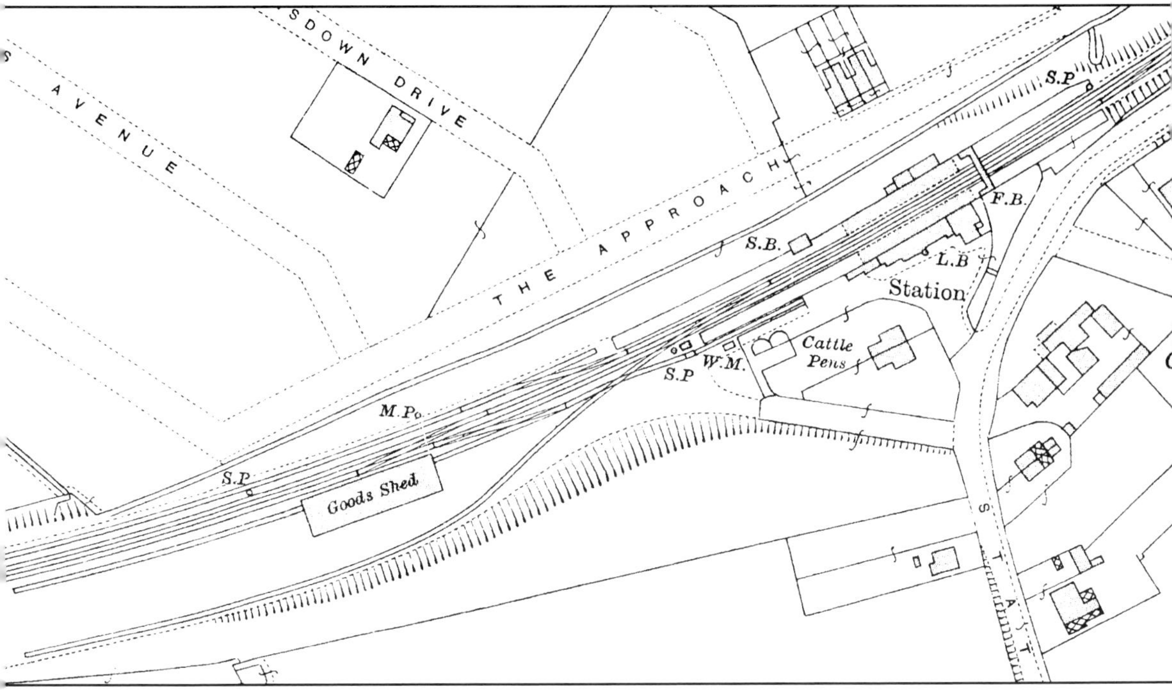

VII. We continue our journey to Southend on the section of route which was doubled in 1901-02. The population rose from 1773 to 20,290 in the subsequent 60 years. There was a private halt west of the station called "Bridge 774", from May 1922 until April 1925. It was used by workers building the Southend Arterial Road, the A127 (T) now.

28. The south elevation faced the approach road and was the subject of an early postcard, along with typical connecting road transport. (P.Laming coll.)

29. An eastward panorama has the signal box on the left. It has limited visibility to the east and the bush will soon restrict it to the west, if not trimmed. (P.Laming coll.)

30. A westward view includes the goods shed and all passengers with hats. Well tended gardens and lack of litter are noteworthy features. (P.Laming coll.)

31. In its last full year of operation a B12 emits steam from improper places, as it runs under the new protective panels on the footbridge. There was a down refuge siding until 1983. (T.Wright/D. Brennand coll.)

32. A view towards Southend soon after electrification includes a staff crossing, a dangerous facility on a curve. All the structures were still functioning over 50 years later. East of the station, there had earlier been a siding at Downhall for a brickworks. Banner repeater signals were provided for both platforms, owing to their curvature. (Norfolk Rly. Soc.)

HOCKLEY

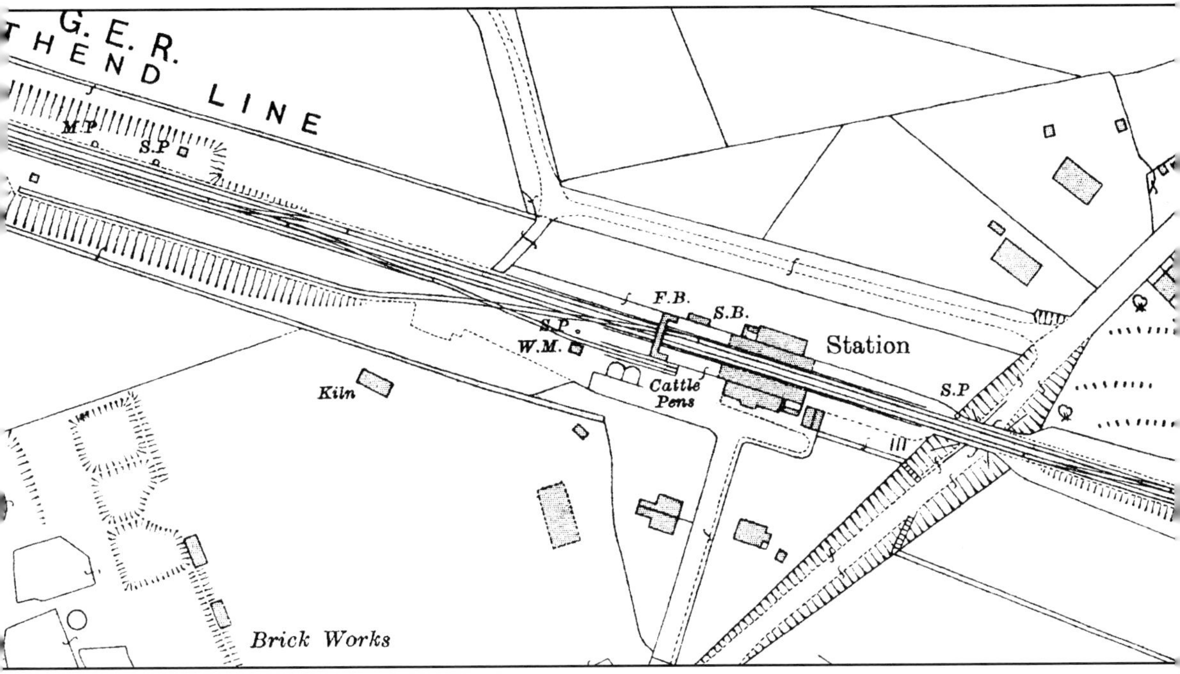

VIII. Few dwellings were nearby at the time of the 1922 survey. There were only 905 souls resident in 1901. There was a public siding east of the station at Hawkwell for many years.

33. The local taxi service left material in the road to benefit rhubarb growers, while others left their transport against the station wall. The parcels shed is in the background. (P.Laming coll.)

34. Staff seem to outnumber passengers in this postcard view, which shows the trailing connection to the goods yard via a crossover. This arrangement reduced facing points on running lines. (P.Laming coll.)

35. Seen from a train running wrong line towards Shenfield on 19th March 1955 is the east elevation of the parcels shed. All structures other than this one remained standing in 2010. (H.C.Casserley)

36. Class J20/1 no. 64680 was recorded shunting the yard in April 1955. The ground frame is just beyond the loading gauge. Freight traffic ceased here on 5th June 1967; a 30cwt crane had been provided in later years. (B.Pask)

37. A panorama from 23rd July 1995 reveals that the footbridge had been fitted with panels to deter mischief makers. The line is over 100ft above sea level here, high for Essex. (B.W.L.Brooksbank)

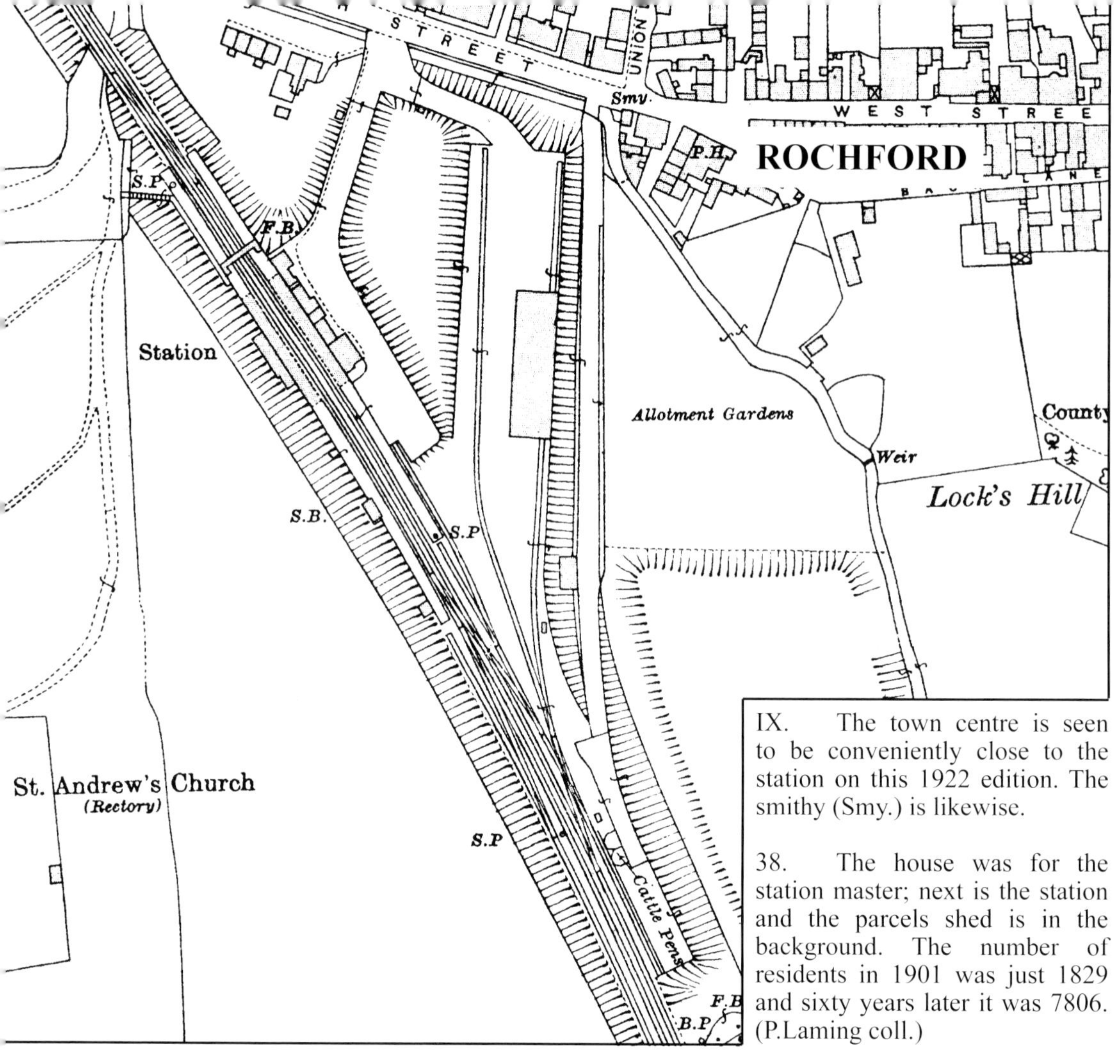

IX. The town centre is seen to be conveniently close to the station on this 1922 edition. The smithy (Smy.) is likewise.

38. The house was for the station master; next is the station and the parcels shed is in the background. The number of residents in 1901 was just 1829 and sixty years later it was 7806. (P.Laming coll.)

39. We are looking southeast with waiting passengers on both platforms. At the foot of the steps on the upside a member of staff attempts his party piece of balancing a parcel on his head, no doubt by now, to perfection. The Land Company of Cheapside seem to be offering homes at £150 each. (P.Laming coll.)

40. The south end of the station was recorded on another postcard in about 1910. The buildings and canopies remained little changed a century later. (P.Laming coll.)

41. The goods yard was photographed in 1959 and was closed on 5th June 1967. The goods shed remained standing in 2010 and was in commercial use. (B.Pask)

42. A train bound for Southend was recorded at the end of the steam era. Even the water column had been dismembered. The air pump is leaking a little steam. (T.Wright/D.Brennand coll.)

PRITTLEWELL

43. A northward panorama from around 1910 shows the now familiar group of buildings, all of which still exist, except the parcels shed, left. (A.Ingram coll.)

X. A more compact layout was provided here, as displayed on this 1922 map. The population was recorded as 2745 in 1901 and 12,094 in 1961. This was due to Southend spreading northwards.

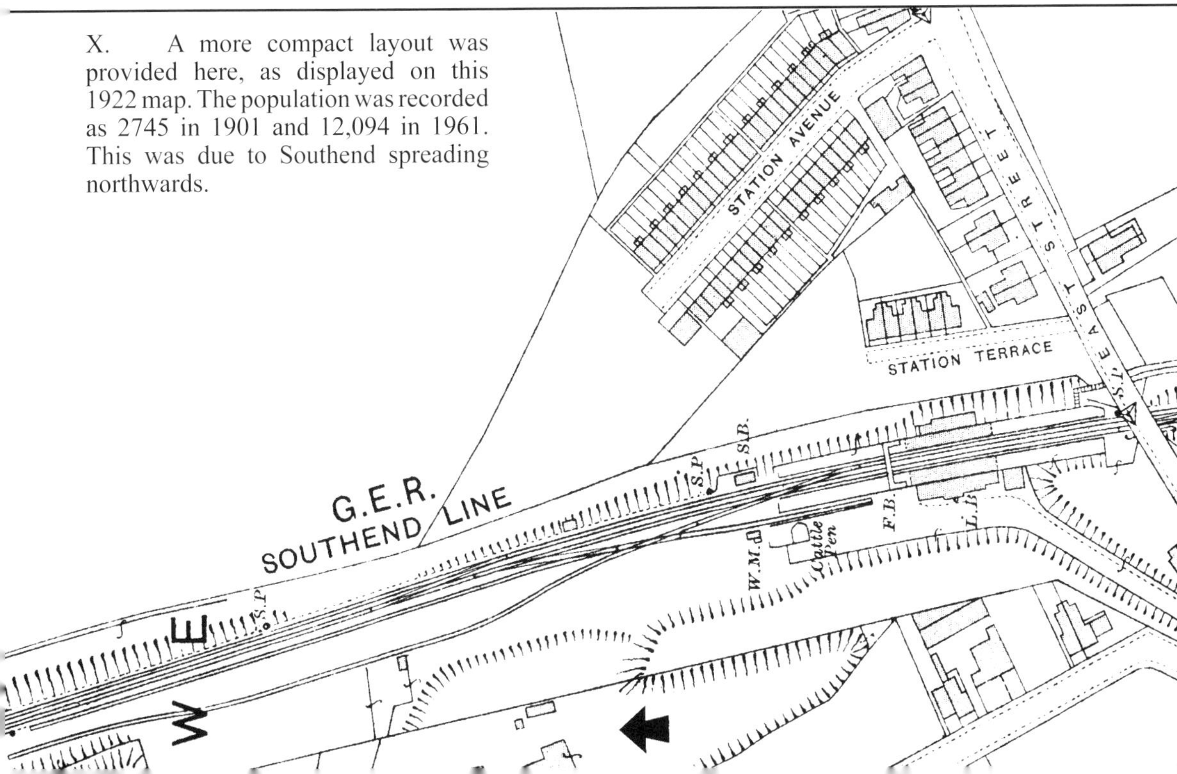

44. The busy yard was photographed in about 1910 from alongside the signal box. Domestic coal was the main traffic. All freight ceased here on 5th June 1967. (R.Hilton/HMRS)

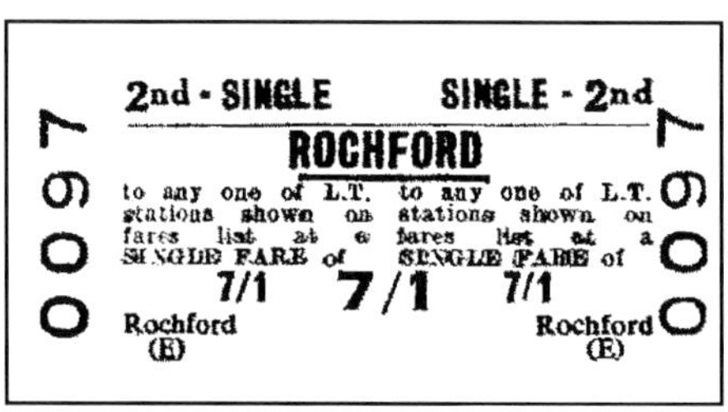

0097
2nd - SINGLE SINGLE - 2nd
ROCHFORD
to any one of L.T. stations shown on fares list at a SINGLE FARE of
to any one of L.T. stations shown on fares list at a SINGLE FARE of
7/1 7/1 7/1
Rochford (E)
Rochford (E)
0097

06 JUN 1964
14680
SINGLE
Rochford Station to
SOUTHEND AIRPORT
BY OMNIBUS
(E)
1/-
For conditions see over
11171

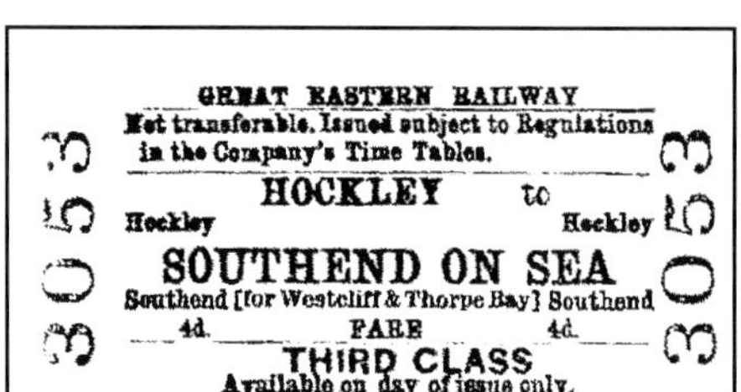

3053
GREAT EASTERN RAILWAY
Not transferable. Issued subject to Regulations in the Company's Time Tables.
HOCKLEY to
Hockley
Hockley
SOUTHEND ON SEA
Southend [for Westcliff & Thorpe Bay] Southend
4d. FARE 4d.
THIRD CLASS
Available on day of issue only.
3053

9399
GREAT EASTERN RAILWAY
Not transferable. Issued subject to Regulations in the Company's Time Tables.
PRITTLEWELL to
Prittlewell
Prittlewell
SOUTHEND ON SEA
Southend [For Westcliff & Thorpe Bay] Southend
1d FARE 1d
THIRD CLASS
Available on day of issue only
9399

45. The station is on the left as class B12/3 4-6-0 no. 61579 approaches its destination with the 1.13pm from Liverpool Street on 2nd July 1955. The northern extremity of the carriage sidings is on the right. (P.J.Kelley)

46. A class L1 is passing through Prittlewell hauling new electric stock dead. L1s were used as they were air braked and so were compatible with the electric stock. A previous attempt to haul stock using a vacuum braked diesel loco had resulted in a runaway and subsequent collision with another train. (B.Pask)

NORTH OF SOUTHEND

47. The locomotive depot is seen in July 1949, with two B12 4-6-0s and an L1 2-6-4T. The allocation in January 1922 was ten 4-4-0s, two 2-4-0s and three 0-6-0s. The water tank is centre. (P.J.Kelley)

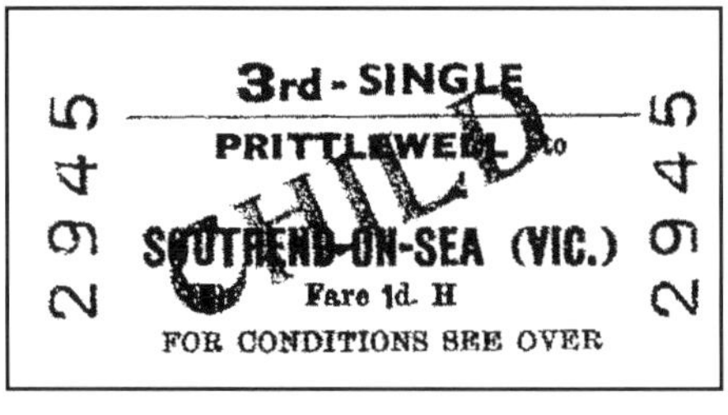

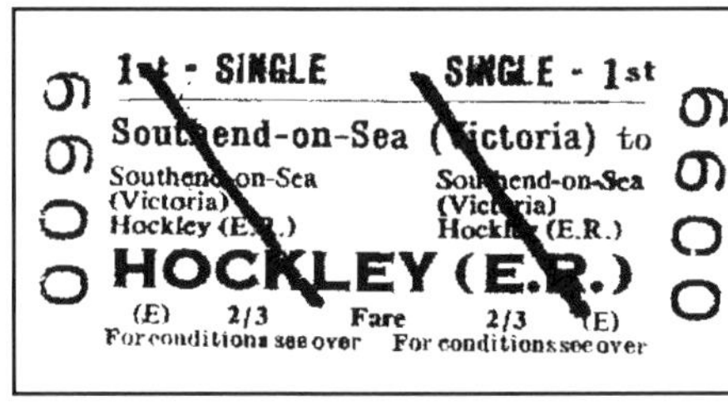

48. The line drops inland at 1 in 100, while the sidings on the left are level. Class B12/3 4-6-0 no. 61579 departs with the 3.54pm to Liverpool Street on 2nd July 1955. (P.J.Kelley)

49. There were seven 4-4-2Ts, fourteen 4-6-0s, five 0-6-0s and four 0-6-2Ts shedded here in October 1954. Standing near the coaling plant on 19th March 1955 are 0-6-2T no. 65721 and 0-6-0 no. 64681. (H.C.Casserley)

50. The shed was sub to Stratford and was coded 30D in the final years. It closed on 30th December 1956. No. 61549 accelerates the 2.36pm to London on 19th March 1955. (H.C.Casserley)

51. Diesel hauled passenger trains were uncommon and usually comprised excursions from beyond the wires. These two class 20s had travelled from the London Midland Region sometime in the 1959-60 period. (D.Brennand coll.)

52. The goods yard closed on 5th June 1967 and it became a Co-op coal concentration depot and was provided with no. D2184, a class 03 diesel shunter. The site functioned until 1986. (D.Brennand)

53. Some of the electrified carriage sidings were recorded on 27th July 1988 with class 302s on the left and 312s on the right. This area was known as "The Klondyke". (F.Hornby)

SOUTHEND VICTORIA

XI. The extent of the four platforms and the three engine release roads is evident on this 1922 edition at 20ins to 1 mile. Two cranes are shown; five-ton loads could be lifted. The goods yard site eventually received extensive premises for the Royal Mail, which were initially served by a siding. A mail train ran to Crewe each night from here. A carriage washing plant was erected in 1982. A reservoir supplied the GER's needs.

54. Running across the picture is Victoria Avenue complete with its tramtrack and setts. A man sporting a superb white cap waits, maybe for one of the trams and a babe enjoys its ride in a three wheeled push chair propelled by humans. Horses take care of larger loads elsewhere. The suffix "For Westcliffe & Thorpe Bay" was used in 1933-49. (P.Laming coll.)

The trams and pier railway are illustrated in *Southend-on-Sea Tramways*.
The line through Southend Central is featured in another Middleton Press album, *Barking to Southend*.
This includes the route to Shoeburyness.

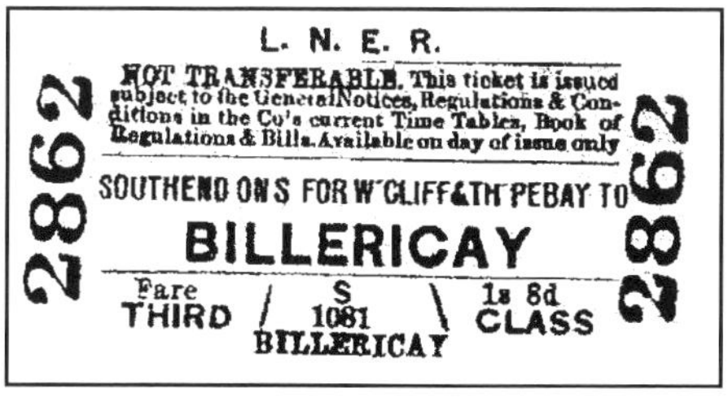

← 55. Platforms 3 and 4 were photographed on 19th March 1955 as the end of steam was nigh. The words "-on-Sea Victoria" had been added on 1st May 1949. The "-on-Sea" was lost on 20th February 1969 for the benefit of the computers then evolving. (H.C.Casserley)

56. A northward panorama in the transition phase includes the signal box, which operated colour light signals from 27th February 1938. (Norfolk Rly. Soc.)

SOUTHEND-ON-SEA
VICTORIA
LIVERPOOL ST
28s

2D51
510

← 57. A class 307 unit is seen soon after electrification, before the application of yellow ends. The steam hauled stock in the background had been introduced with a finish intended to represent varnished teak. The four lights acted as route indicators, as on the tube lines of London Transport. (D.Brennand coll.)

← 58. At platform 2 on 6th April 1976 is no. 510, a second generation EMU, by then classified AM5/2. Buildings rise as litter falls. The 1960 units had pantographs instead of bow collectors. (SLS coll.)

59. Most of the sidings adjacent to the four platforms are evident in this southward view from 7th July 1990. The canopies had been reclad and reglazed in 1986. On the right are nos 321306 and 321362. (B.I.Nathan)

60. National Express East Anglia-liveried no. 321308 awaits departure on 13th October 2009, forming the 10.26 service to London Liverpool Street. The centre release road had long gone, but the cast iron stanchions and their fine tracery brackets had been retained. (B.Morrison)

2. Battlesbridge to Maldon

BATTLESBRIDGE

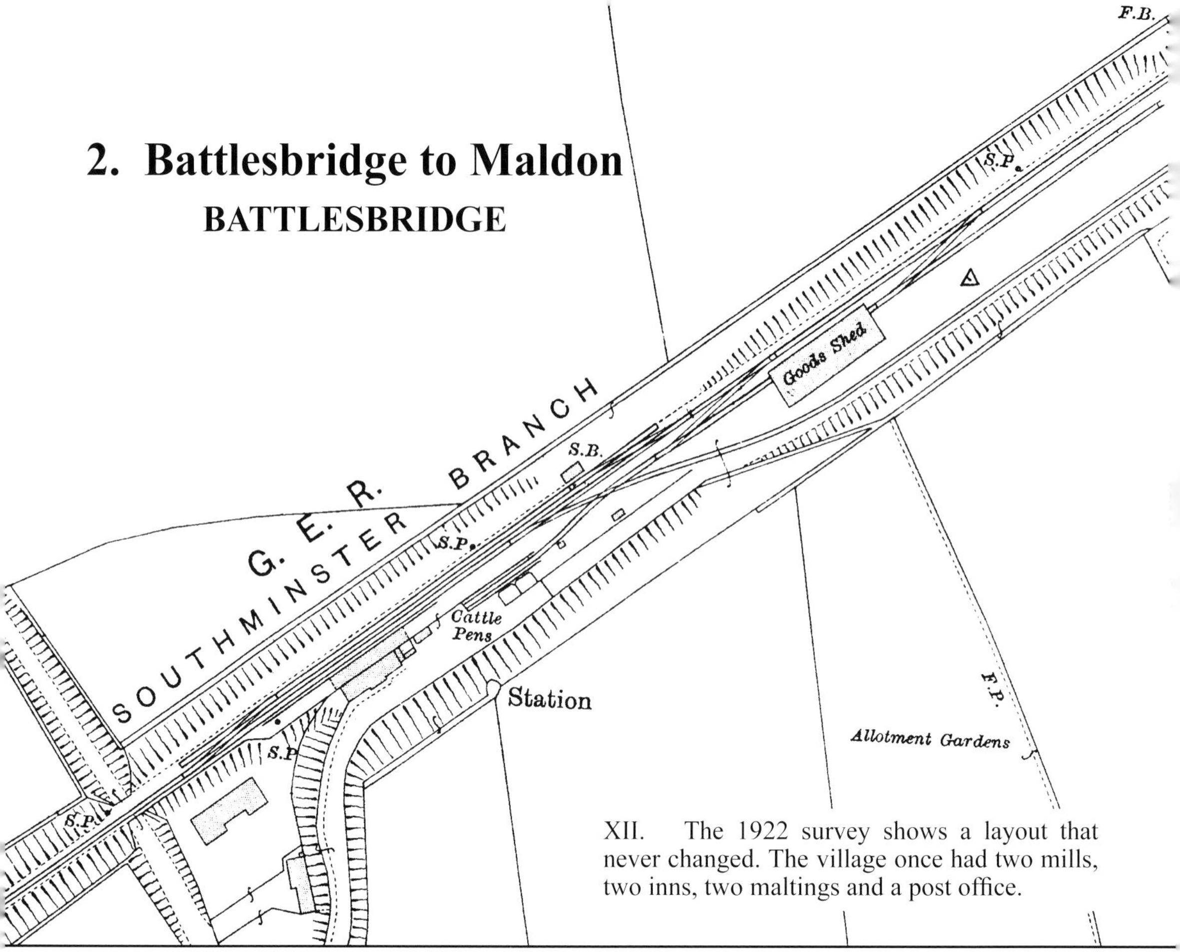

XII. The 1922 survey shows a layout that never changed. The village once had two mills, two inns, two maltings and a post office.

61. This was a charming secluded rural station in a very peaceful location, remote from habitation. Inset is the World War I propoganda poster displayed in the window. (P.Laming coll.)

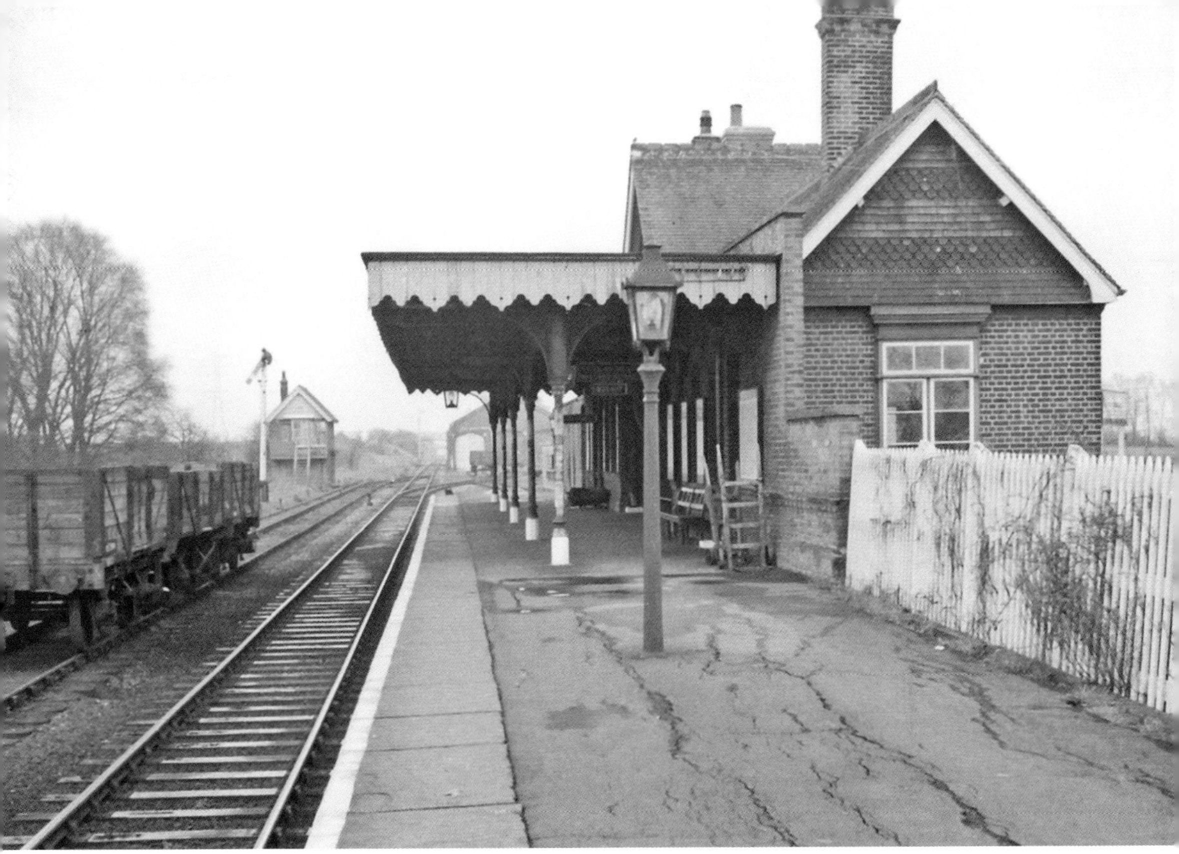

62. An eastward view on 9th April 1961 shows that the loop was for goods traffic only. Its west end is included on the front cover and freight service was withdrawn on 4th October 1965. The loop was taken out of use on 7th December 1966. The 34-lever signal box was closed that day. (B.W.L.Brooksbank)

63. All buildings were destroyed in 1968 and this westward picture is from 8th June 1969. The platform has been lengthened subsequently to take eight car trains. (H.C.Casserley)

SOUTH WOODHAM FERRERS

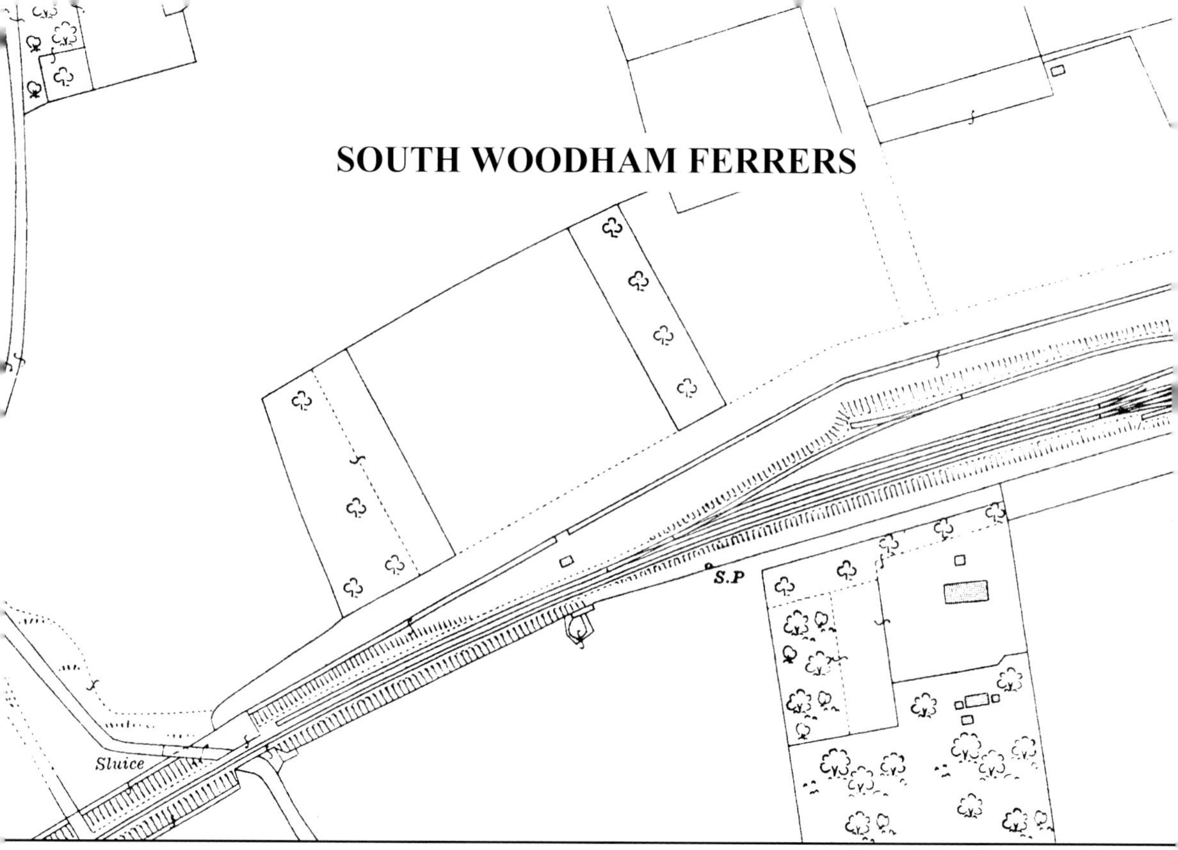

XIII. The 1922 map emphasises the great length of the goods yard, which includes a loop but no crane. A turntable had been used by the Maldon engines until 1911. The Maldon and Southminster lines diverge on the right on an area now covered in houses.

64. Wicker baskets abound in this postcard view eastwards. One would expect the signal box to be nearer to the level crossing and the junction. Woodham Ferrers housed 878 folk in 1901 and 2215 in 1961. (P.Laming coll.)

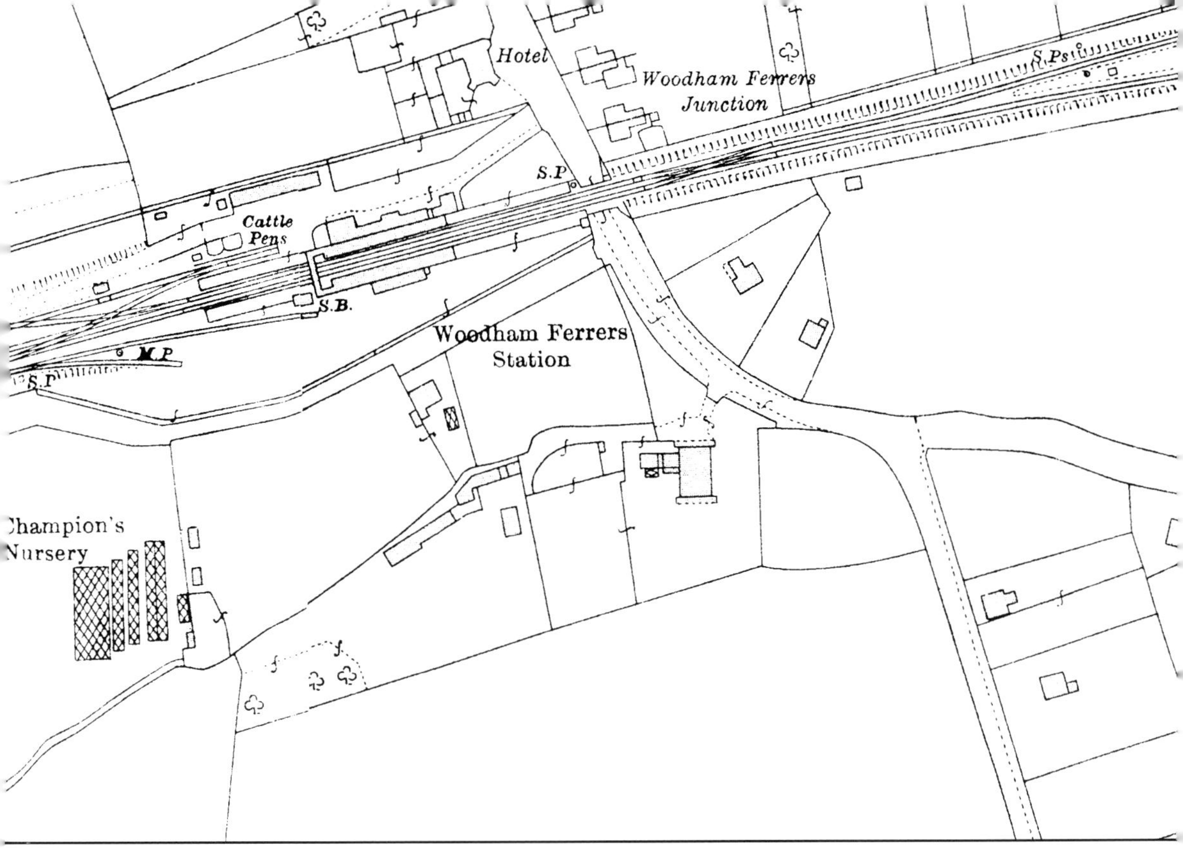

65. The junction signals are at the end of the down platform, on the left. There was a small hut available for the crossing keeper until "automatic open" status was provided on 9th March 1986. After many complaints, automatic half barriers came into use on 4th April 1993. (P.Laming coll.)

66. Familiar architecture is featured in another early postcard, the photograph having been taken from the level crossing. The spelling was "Ferris" until 1st October 1913 and "South" was added on 20th May 2007. (P.Laming coll.)

67. The level crossing is in the background in this record of 0-6-2T class N7/4 no. 69613 working a train from Southminster, sometime in the 1950s. (W.A.Camwell/SLS coll.)

68. The loop and 36-lever signal box were taken out of use on 21st January 1967 and soon removed. The station was photographed on 8th June 1969 and part of it was still in use for ticket sales in 2010 on Monday to Friday mornings. We now take a journey up the little used line to Maldon. (H.C.Casserley)

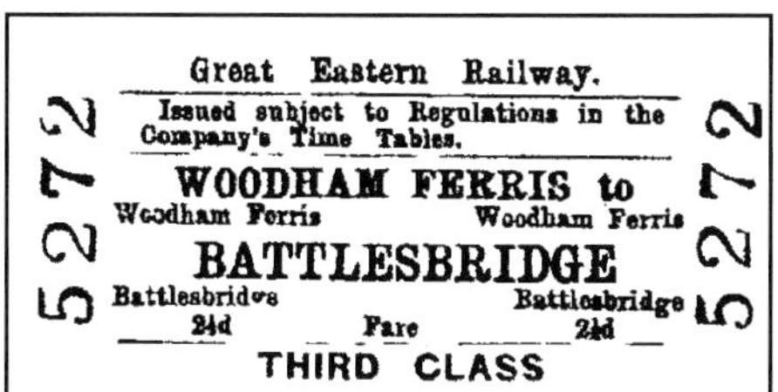

Great Eastern Railway.
Issued subject to Regulations in the Company's Time Tables.
WOODHAM FERRIS to
Woodham Ferris Woodham Ferris
BATTLESBRIDGE
Battlesbridge
2½d Fare 2½d
THIRD CLASS
5272 5272

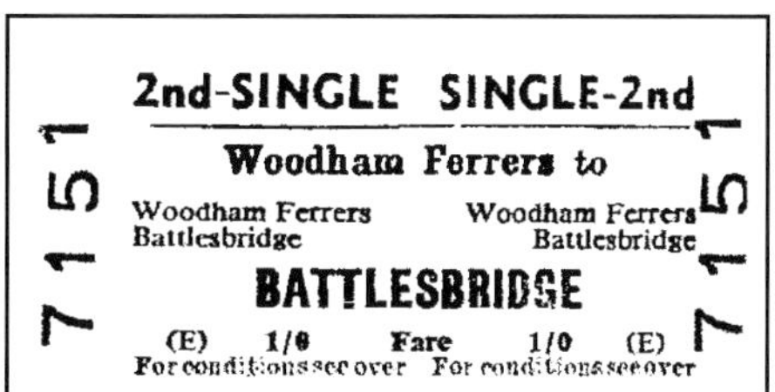

2nd-SINGLE SINGLE-2nd
Woodham Ferrers to
Woodham Ferrers Woodham Ferrers
Battlesbridge Battlesbridge
BATTLESBRIDGE
(E) 1/0 Fare 1/0 (E)
For conditions see over For conditions see over
7151 7151

STOW ST. MARY HALT

69. This stop came into use on 24th September 1928 and this snap was taken in its final year, 1939. The village of Stow Maries was ¼ mile to the north, but it was reported that the halt was named differently at the insistence of the vicar. (Neaves/ Maldon District Museum)

XIV. The 1ins to 1 mile map, revised in 1952-55, shows no trace of the halt, but marks Cold Norton as closed, with an open circle. The route south of it was closed during World War II and used for wagon storage.

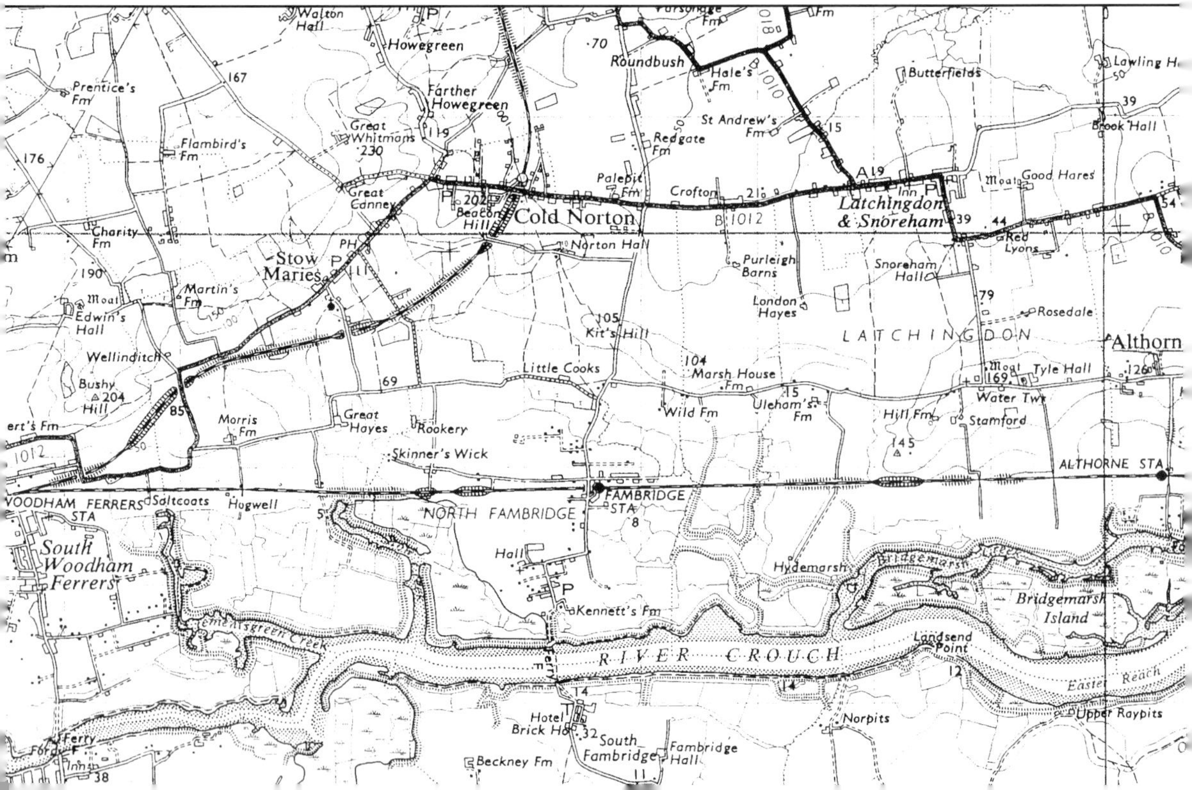

COLD NORTON

70. The full range of facilities was provided, despite the low number of residents. On the left are the cattle pens and the open door is on the parcels shed. (P.Laming coll.)

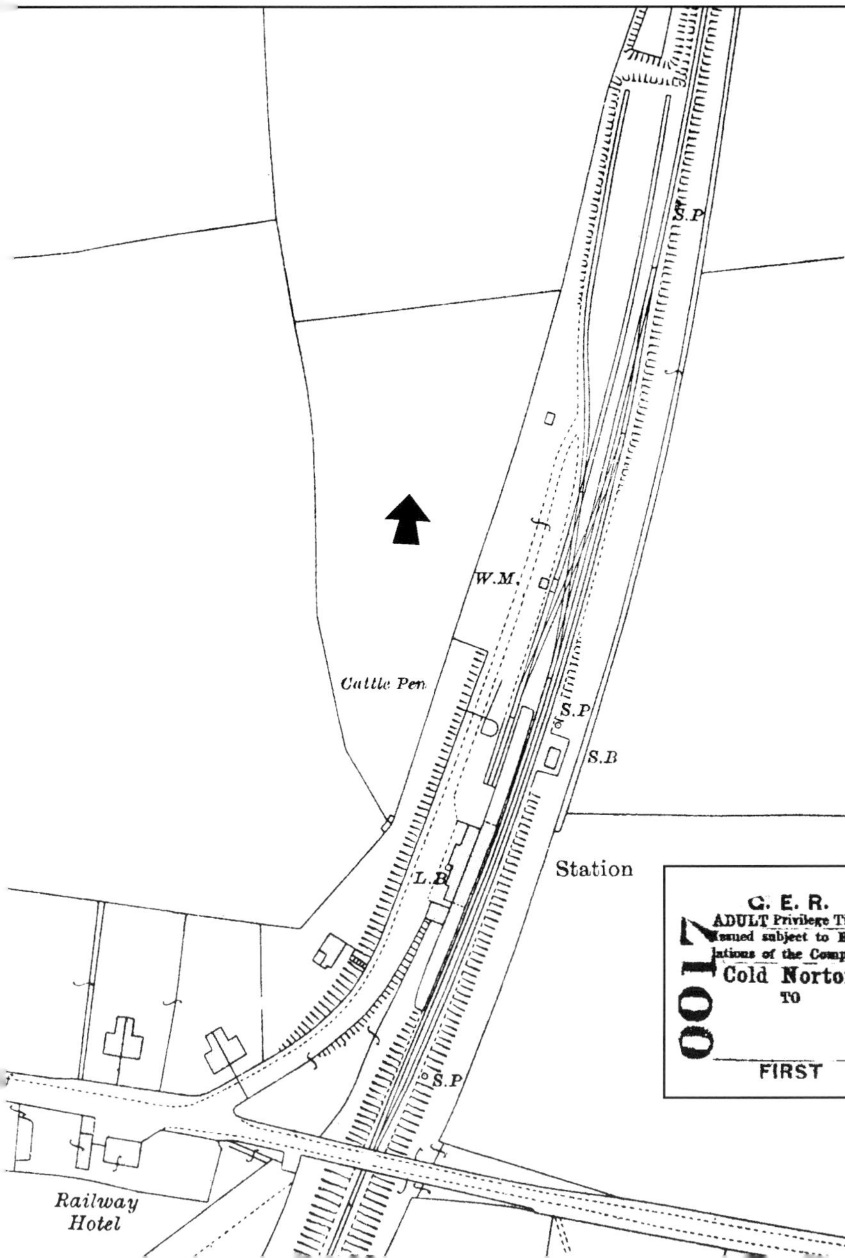

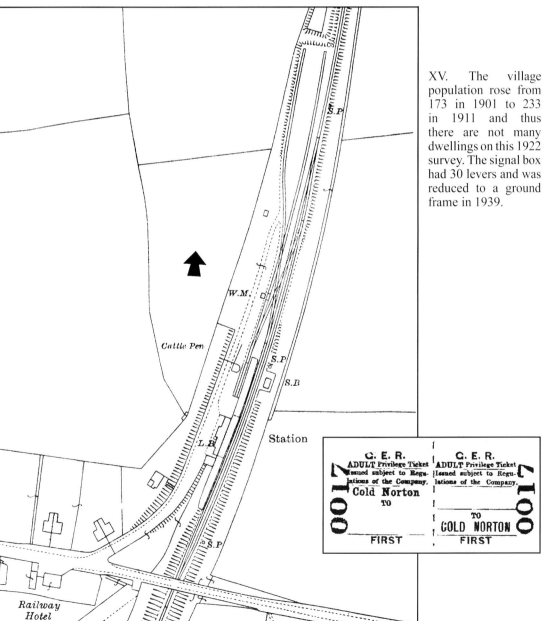

XV. The village population rose from 173 in 1901 to 233 in 1911 and thus there are not many dwellings on this 1922 survey. The signal box had 30 levers and was reduced to a ground frame in 1939.

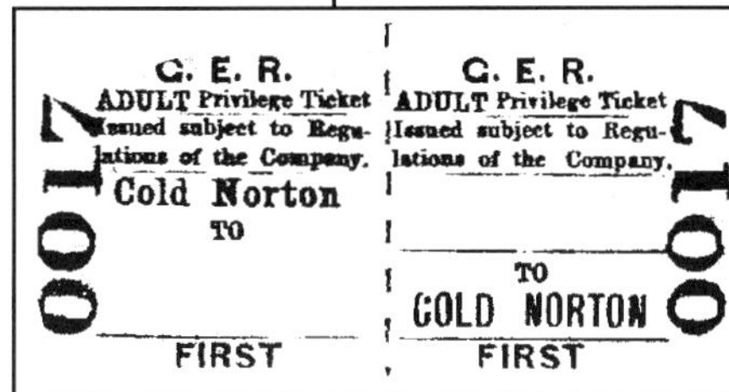

71. The loop line was freight only and this service lasted until 1st April 1953, passenger traffic on the route ceasing in September 1939. (SLS coll.)

72. The running-in board now proclaims that the station no longer serves Purleigh and Stow Maries and has adopted Latchington, no doubt to the signwriter's relief. Two lads make up for the lack of passengers, one viewing the photographer. The platform no longer offers the image of a busy station and has adopted an overall run down appearance. (P.Laming coll.)

BARON'S LANE HALT

73. Here is the porter-in-charge in the 1930s, together with the local coal merchant, plus his horse and cart. The halt is mentioned in the 1937 Baedeker's Guide to Great Britain. (Lacey/Maldon District Museum)

74. The sidings came into use with the line, but the halt did not open until 10th July 1922. Freight traffic ceased on 1st April 1953. (Great Eastern Society)

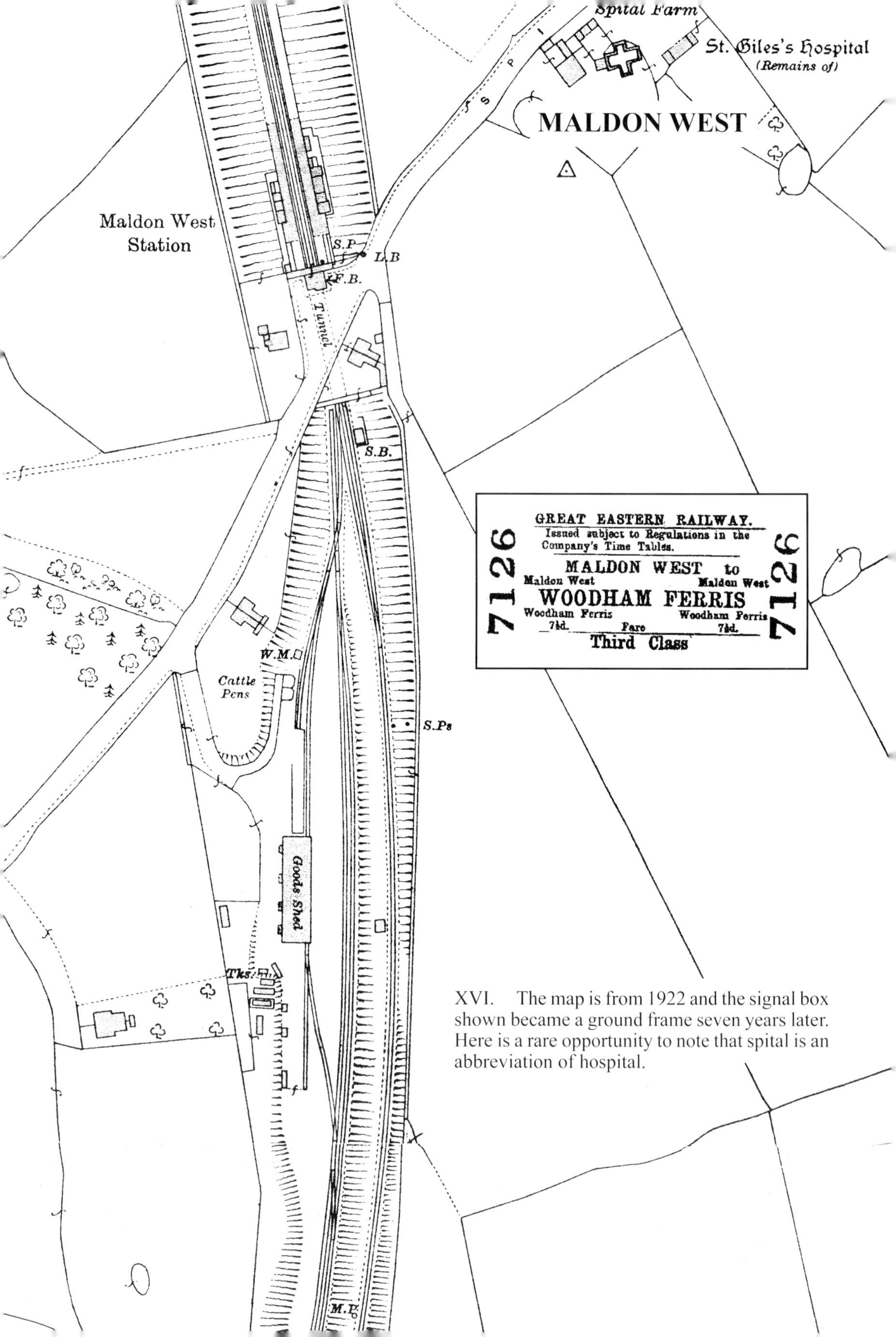

XVI. The map is from 1922 and the signal box shown became a ground frame seven years later. Here is a rare opportunity to note that spital is an abbreviation of hospital.

75. The crowd gives the impression of a busy station, but it was beyond the fringe of the town. This is the south elevation in around 1910. The station was closed to passengers from 28th May 1916 to 1st February 1919. (P.Laming coll.)

76. The north elevation was recorded in about 1950. The goods yard was beyond the tunnel and closed on 1st September 1954, but was open again from 31st January 1957 until 31st June 1959. This area is now under a roundabout and the A414 takes the railway alignment as far as the former junction, north of the town. (R.M.Casserley coll.)

77. Few passengers alighted here after 1939, but an exception was recorded on 6th April 1957 when a railtour called. The locomotive is class J67/2 0-6-0T no. 68628 with a Railway Enthusiasts Club trip, which started at Witham and included Kelvedon, with open wagons to Tiptree and back. (E.Wilmshurst)

NORTH OF MALDON

78. On leaving Maldon West, trains crossed two bridges. The first was over the tidal River Chelmer and is seen in August 1961. The second was over a navigable link. (J.H.Meredith)

79. The line straight ahead is to Witham and the one to Maldon West curves to the left. It had been singled in 1924 and was subject to a 15mph speed limit. It was used for wagon storage in the late 1950s. This was the second of two bridges over the Chelmer & Blackwater Navigation. (Dr. J.Westall/A.H.Vaughan coll.)

80. We move nearer to Maldon East station and look towards the junction from the level crossing. In the foreground is an underpass, with only 9ft headroom, which could be used when the gates were closed. The sidings on the right ran to the canal. The box had 62 levers, was closed on 18th April 1966 and demolished in November 1979. (Dr. J.Westall/A.H.Vaughan coll.)

MALDON EAST & HEYBRIDGE

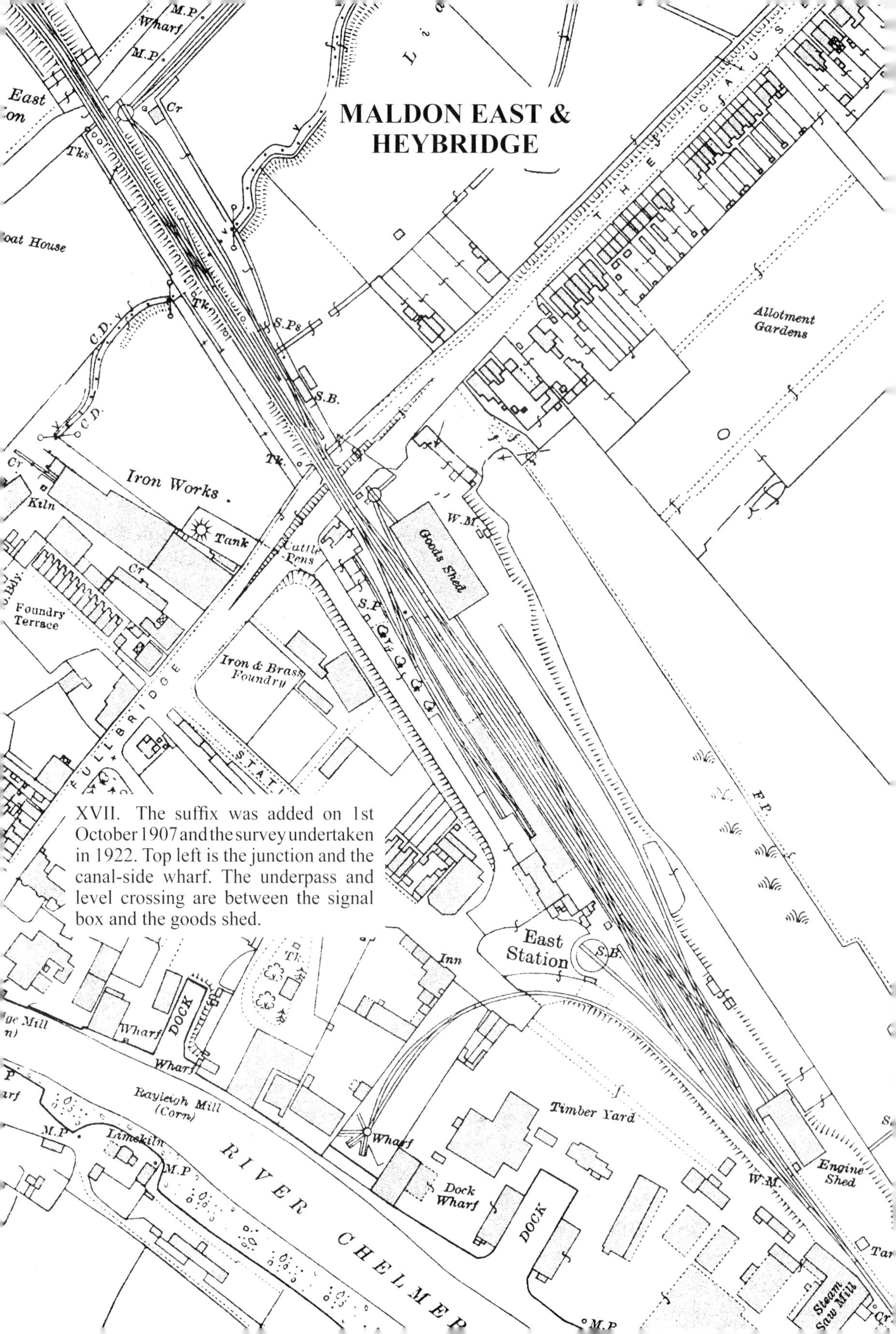

XVII. The suffix was added on 1st October 1907 and the survey undertaken in 1922. Top left is the junction and the canal-side wharf. The underpass and level crossing are between the signal box and the goods shed.

81. The impressive station opened on 2nd October 1848 and is now a listed structure. The Jacobean style included a nine-arch colonnade and the gabled pavilions, which were designed to impress for political reasons at the time. (P.Laming coll.)

82. The view south in the 1950s includes the two-road engine shed on the left. This was a sub-shed of Colchester (30E) and five 2-4-2Ts were listed here in 1922. It closed with the advent of dieselisation. (D.Brennand coll.)

83. DMUs ran on the branch to Witham from 14th June 1956, thus the railtour seen first in picture 77 was one of the last trains to be steam hauled. The skyline is worthy of study in this and the next picture. (A.Attwell/H.Davies)

84. DMUs gave way to four-wheeled diesel railbuses on 7th July 1958. The Eastern Region had five built in Germany by Waggon und Maschinenbau. This specimen is seen on 29th November 1963; they ran here until closure on 7th September 1964. Freight continued until 18th April 1966. (E.Wilmshurst)

3. Crouch Valley Line
to Southminster
NORTH FAMBRIDGE

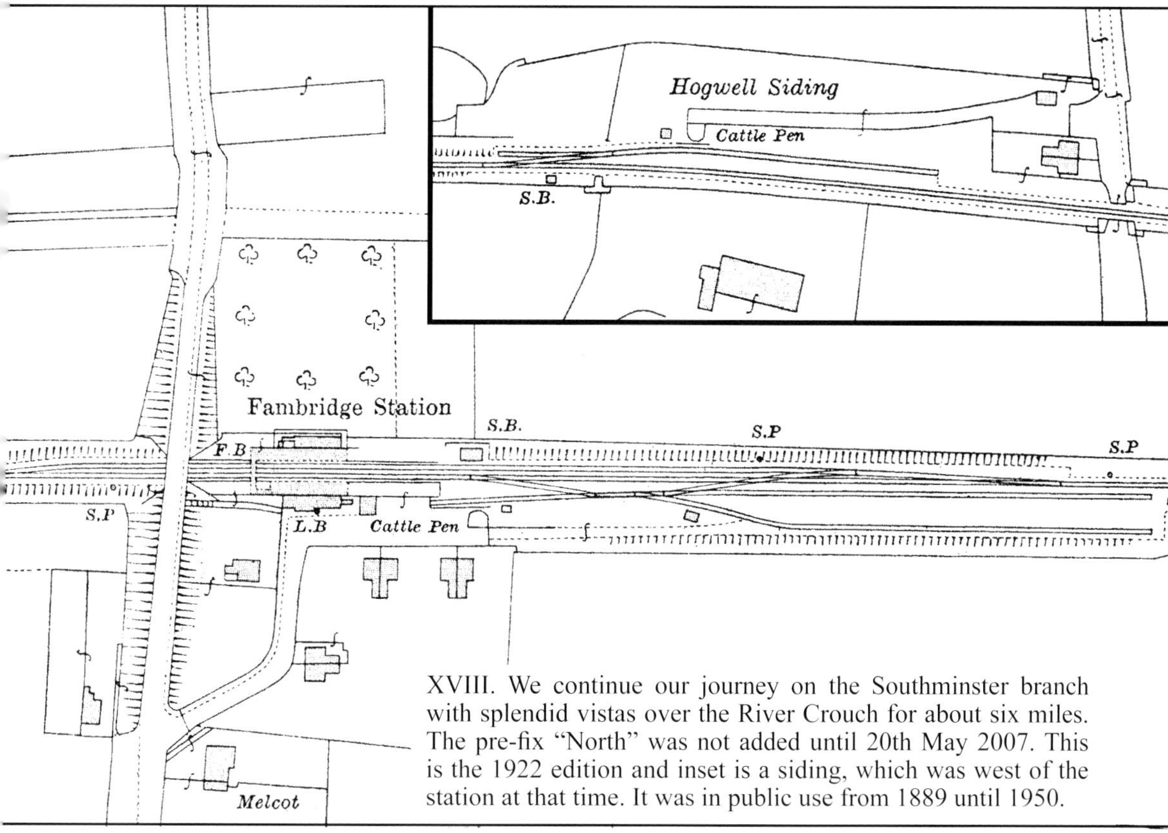

XVIII. We continue our journey on the Southminster branch with splendid vistas over the River Crouch for about six miles. The pre-fix "North" was not added until 20th May 2007. This is the 1922 edition and inset is a siding, which was west of the station at that time. It was in public use from 1889 until 1950.

85. We look east and have the goods yard in the right distance. Until the 1950s, one could walk south for a mile and then take a ferry across the Crouch to South Fambridge. (SLS coll.)

86. There were ten levers in the signal box, which closed on 1st December 1985 and was demolished in February 1986. It had 30 levers until 1966. A rare speck of litter ruins this postcard view of a train arriving from Southminster. (P.Laming coll.)

87. The blind on this DMU indicates where it had started its journey. It is early in its life, as the cats whiskers are still on display. (Norfolk Rly. Soc.)

88. An eastward panorama on 14th May 1974 is from the footbridge, which was replaced with one at a higher level prior to electrification. The roofless gents and redundant parcels shed remain. The track is straight for almost three miles. (SLS coll.)

89. All was cleared away, but eventually funds were found for bricks for the two buildings photographed on 30th August 1992. The platforms were lengthened and trains pass here almost every hour, the loop being controlled from Liverpool Street. (B.W.L.Brooksbank)

ALTHORNE

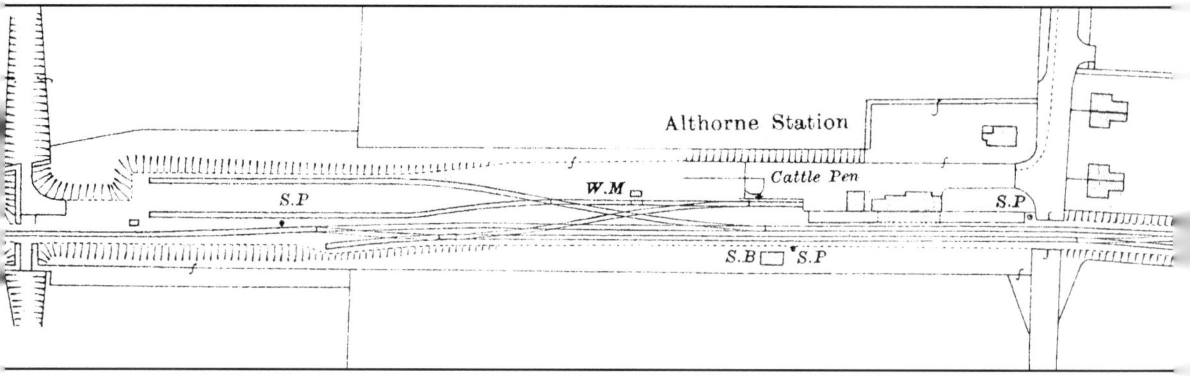

XIX. The station was the most isolated on the route and was at the end of a rough lane, almost one mile from the village. This housed 338 souls in 1901 and still only 483 in 1961. The map is from 1922.

90. A westward panorama prior to 1920 features the impeccable gardens, which won numerous awards over the years. The loop was for goods only and the platform held five coaches. (P.Laming coll.)

91. The goods yard is in the distance of this 1960 photograph and it closed on 19th December of that year. The signal box lasted until 21st January 1967; it had 30 levers. (D.Brennand coll.)

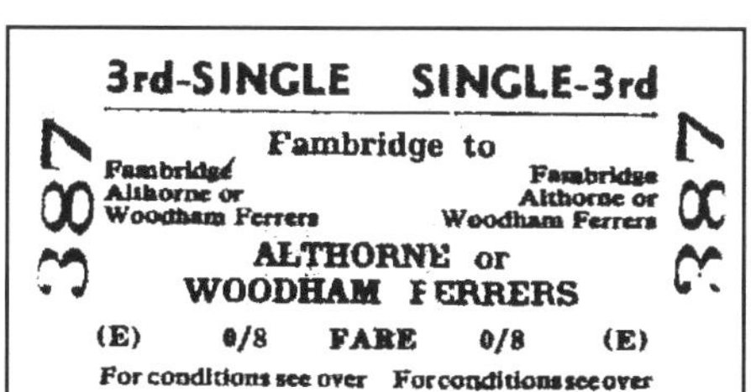

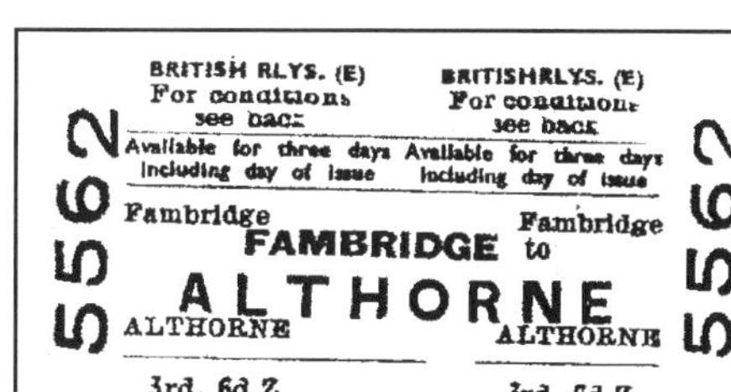

92. The level crossing in the distance was normally locked against road vehicles, but became an automatic open crossing, with lights. The main buildings had gone by the time of this picture from June 1969, leaving the parcels shed and gents. The four ex-railway houses still stand. (H.C.Casserley)

93. The DMU is destined for Wickford in September 1972. The signals protect the level crossing and were worked from a two-lever ground frame. (Colour-Rail)

94. This westward view is from 30th August 1992, with NSE logos on show. The Crouch Valley Line logos appeared later. The platform had been extended for eight coaches in 1987. (B.W.L.Brooksbank)

EAST OF ALTHORNE

XX. This siding was two miles from Althorne and one from Burnham. It received traffic to and from the Creeksea Ferry. The map is from 1922; the operational period was 1889 to 1947.

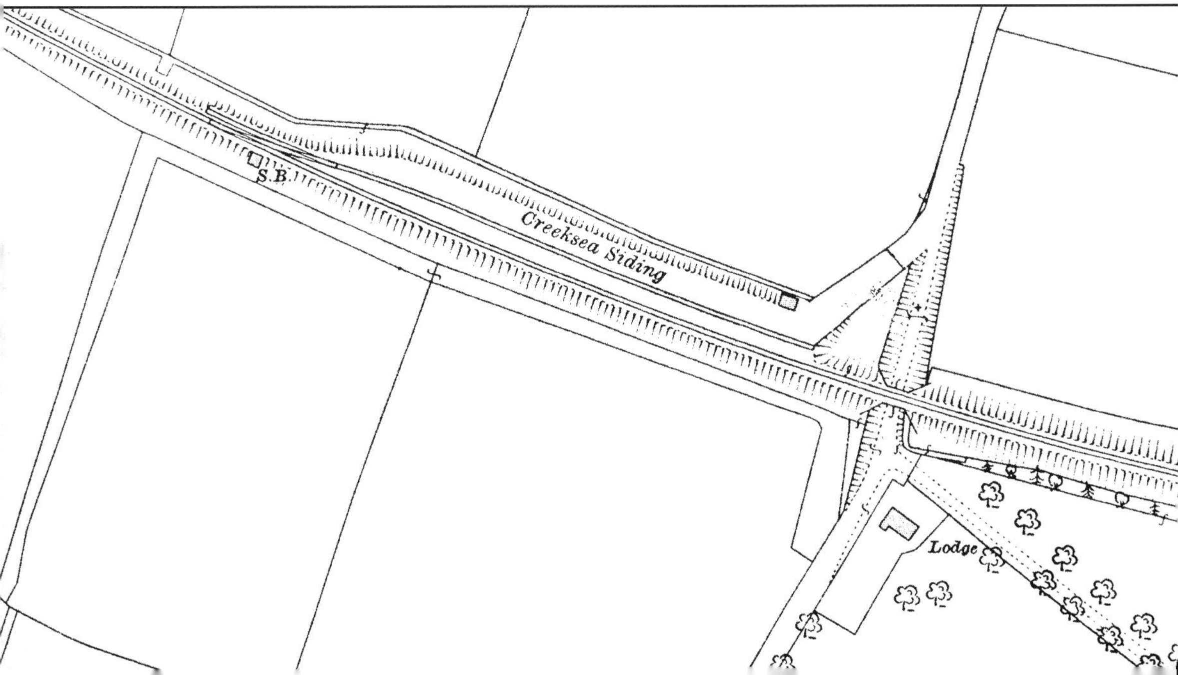

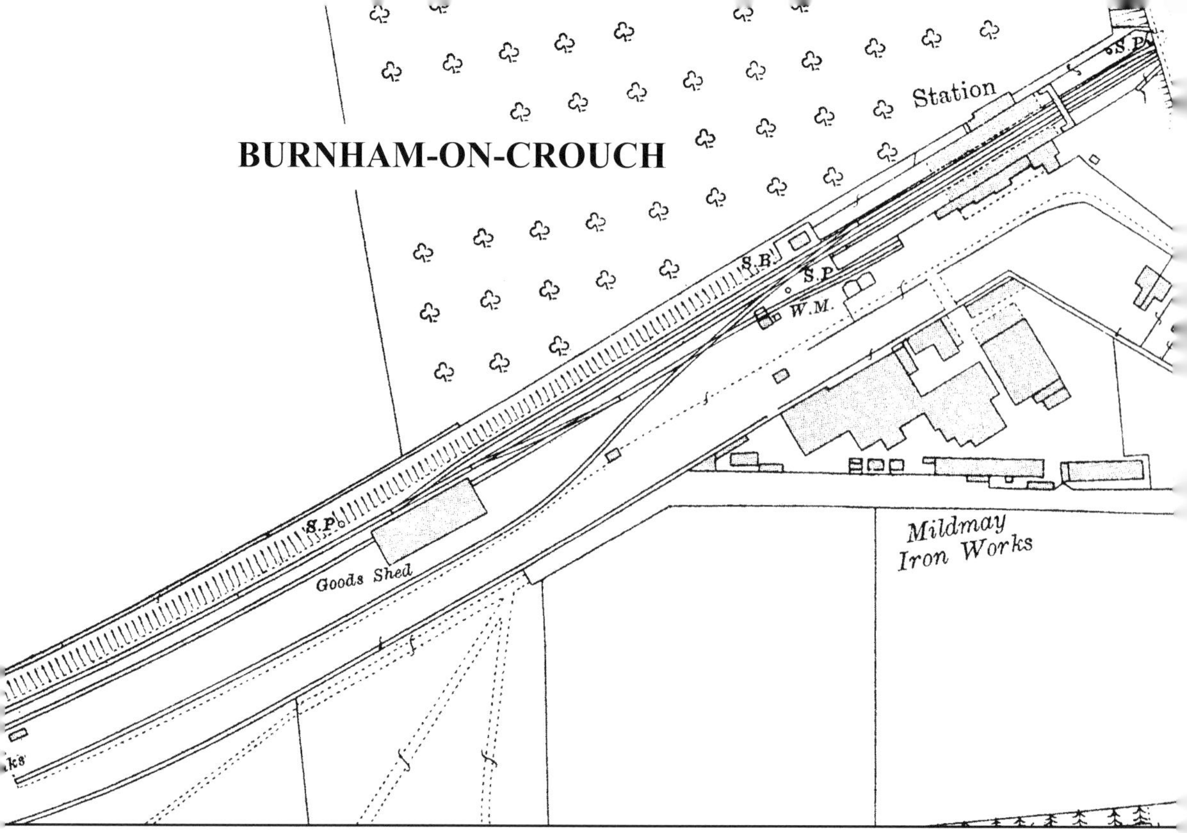

XXI. The 1922 edition includes the long established foundry, which generated much goods traffic. Coal and ore probably came in by sea in the early years. There was a 30cwt crane in the goods shed; a 3-ton one was provided in the yard in later years.

95. Four trolleys and four men (only two with watch chains) oblige the postcard photographer in about 1900. Handling oyster and fish traffic would be their specialisation. Much sugar beet was loaded in the sidings in the 1950s. (P.Laming coll.)

96. A panorama from April 1961 has a coacting signal in the foreground. The population that year was 4200; it had been 2100 in 1901 and rose to 6300 in 1981. (B.W.L.Brooksbank)

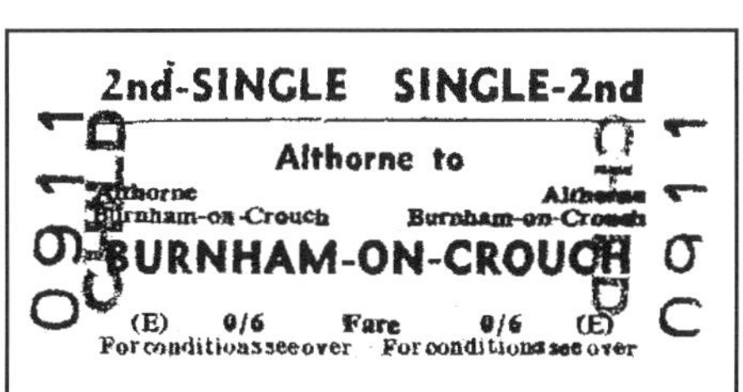

97. The loop and the 24-lever signal box had gone, the latter closing on 21st January 1967. We witness no. D5519 with an up gravel train on 23rd August 1968. (R.F.Roberts/SLS)

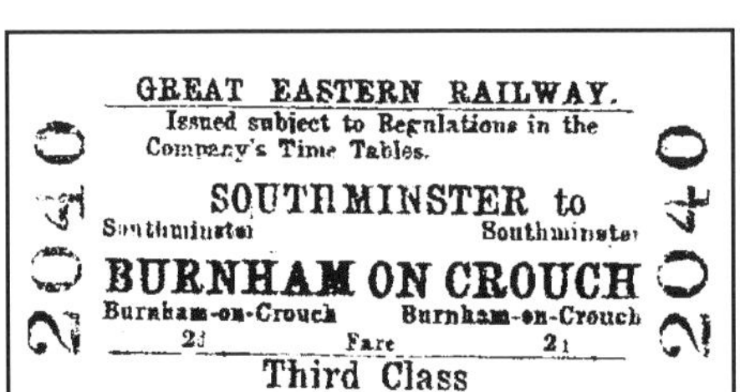

GREAT EASTERN RAILWAY.
Issued subject to Regulations in the Company's Time Tables.
2040
SOUTHMINSTER to
Southminster
Southminster
BURNHAM ON CROUCH
Burnham-on-Crouch
Burnham-on-Crouch
Fare
Third Class
2040

GREAT EASTERN RAILWAY.
Not transferable. Issued subject to Regulations in the Company's Time Tables.
5661
BURNHAM ON CROUCH to
Burnham-on-Crouch
Burnham-on-Crouch
FAMBRIDGE
Fambridge
Fambridge
5d.
FARE
5d
THIRD CLASS
Available on day of issue only
5661

98. The 16.30 service from Wickford to Southminster makes the stop at Burnham on 12th September 1983, led by a Craven class 105 DMU. The disused goods shed is in the background. (B.Morrison)

99. The shabby station is seen at the time of electrification in 1986. Ten years later, there was a major renovation scheme; all the broken windows were boarded up and the exterior painted. A ticket office was in use on Monday to Friday mornings in 2010 and the canopy was still in place. (R.Darsley)

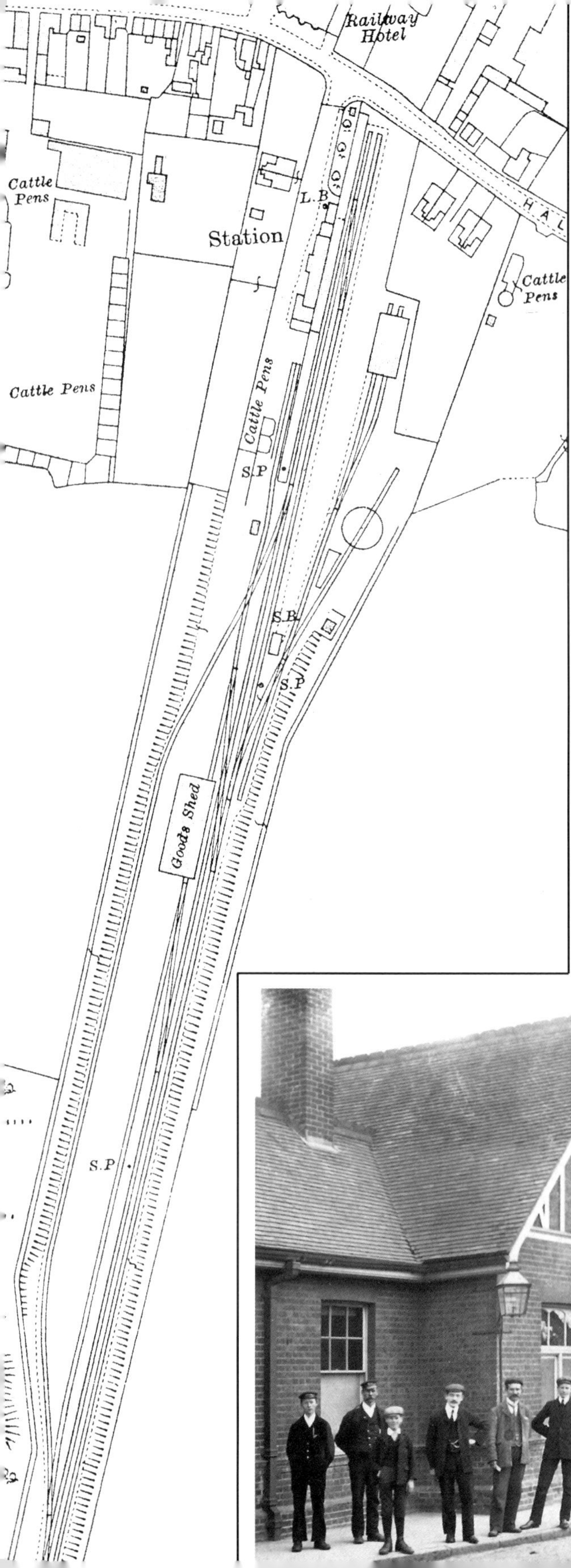

SOUTHMINSTER

XXII. The 1922 survey has gravel pits at the bottom. The left track continued south to serve sidings into them and this traffic continued until 3rd November 1979. The pits shown were dug by the GER and supplied ballast for the construction and maintenance of the line until the early 1920s. The "ballast siding", which was accessed from the headshunt, was then used to accommodate a camping coach until 1939. There was also a private siding, further south off the headshunt, serving Ratsborough Farm. It is thought this was removed before WWII. Commercial gravel traffic started in the early 1950s, from pits south of the former railway pits and also on the east side of the line. Loading took place on the headshunt and there was an overhead conveyor to take gravel across the line from the eastern pits to the screening, washing and loading area.

100. Uniformed workers and clerical staff pose for another postcard. In this we can enjoy intricate porch supports. Population figures were thus: 2130 in 1881, 4200 in 1961 and 6380 in 1981. (P.Laming coll.)

101. A pre-1923 photograph includes the white fence at the end of the line and the bedroom window from which the station master could survey his empire. (SLS coll.)

102. There are no passengers in sight as class N7/3 0-6-2T no. 69703 waits to leave for Wickford at 2.34pm on 21st February 1953. There were devastating floods in the district that year, but the engine shed (right) had been damaged earlier, in 1950. (P.J.Kelley)

103. A panorama from 19th March 1955 has the lamp hut on the left and the water tank on the right. Class B12 4-6-0 no. 61546 has worked a Saturdays-only through train from Liverpool Street and is leaving the shed after turning and watering. (H.C.Casserley)

104. A photograph from 2nd April 1955 reveals that the engine shed walls were repaired, but the roof was never restored. Steam traction ceased in the following year. (R.M.Casserley)

105. Iron ore hopper wagons were present on 3rd August 1968; they were being used for gravel traffic. The material was taken to a former coal depot at Mile End, beyond Stratford. It was mostly sand. (R.F.Roberts/SLS)

106. No. 37247 has arrived with empty gravel wagons on 6th April 1976, while a DMU waits to leave for Wickford at 12.10. Class 37s started on this traffic in 1967 and by 1969 were moving 175,000 tons per annum. (SLS coll.)

GREAT EASTERN RAILWAY.

Not transferable. Issued subject to Regulations in the Company's Time Tables.

3218 SOUTHMINSTER to 3218

Southminster Southminster

BURNHAM ON CROUCH

Burnham-on-Crouch Burnham-on-Crouch

2d. FARE 2d.

8] Third Class

Available on day of issue only.

107. A BR Derby Class 116 DMU with Driving Motor Brake No. E53894 leading, approaches its destination on 12th September 1983, forming the 15.08 service from Wickford. The goods yard had closed on 4th October 1965, but the signal box remained in use until 19th January 1986. It had 36 levers. (B.Morrison)

108. Seen on the same day is the 15.56 departure to Wickford. A ticket office remained in use on workday mornings until 1992. (B.Morrison)

109. A southward view from the platform end on 16th August 2006 shows the running line deviating to the left and the gantry, which was provided in 1962 for nuclear flasks to and from Bradwell Power Station. The wagons were destined for Sellafield and the traffic continued until 31st August 2006. (B.I.Nathan)

110. Turning round, we see one of the well maintained class 321 EMUs and the renovated building in which a room was retained for the comfort of train crew members. (B.I.Nathan)

111. Moving under the canopy, we can marvel that there is an opportunity to frustrate graffiti vandals. They can make no impact on this yellow brick road mural, created in 2004. (B.I.Nathan)

4. Mangapps Railway Museum

112. This is a privately owned working museum established on a farm north of Burnham-on-Crouch. It was created and is owned by John Jolly. It features a standard gauge passenger carrying line, with restored stations, signal boxes and ancillary equipment removed from various sites throughout East Anglia. The train ride is ¾ mile long through the pleasant setting of Mangapps Farm. Passengers can alight at Old Heath Station and take a leisurely stroll along the lineside to the far end of the line. This panorama is from 28th August 1999 and the empty track is adjacent to the passenger platform. (J.M.Jolly)

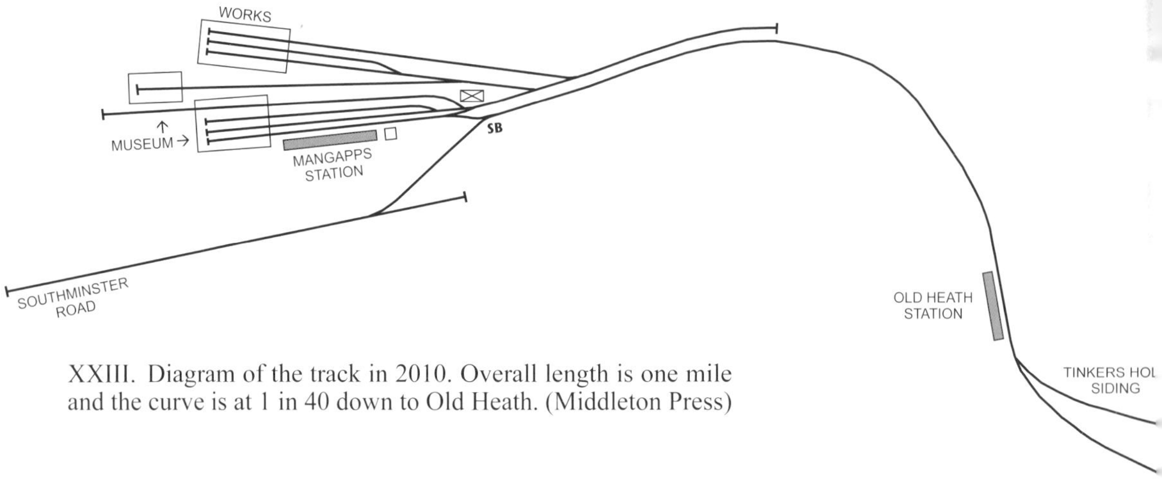

XXIII. Diagram of the track in 2010. Overall length is one mile and the curve is at 1 in 40 down to Old Heath. (Middleton Press)

113. This DMU coach of 1961 is a driving trailer and is propelled by a diesel locomotive on non-steaming days. Mangapps station building on the left came from Horam on the Mid-Suffolk Light Railway. (M.Turvey)

114. The exhibition building contains an astonishing range of exhibits and some are housed in railway vehicles. Many of the items are from stations featured in this album. (P.G.Barnes)

➔ 115. This and most of the following photographs were taken on 29th August 2009, the 20th anniversary of the opening of the museum. It was a diesel gala day and featured here are nos 33207 and 47793. (P.G.Barnes)

➘ 116. No. 03399 is at the rear of a train running into the station. The locomotive was built at Doncaster in 1961 and worked at Ipswich and Colchester. Behind it is class 302 electric stock, which was built at Eastleigh in 1958. There were over 80 items of rolling stock on the site in 2010. (P.G.Barnes)

➘ 117. Bagnall built this 0-6-0ST in 1954 and it was named *Empress*, by the National Coal Board. It worked at Cadley Hall Colliery for most of its life. It carried the name *Demelza* when it was preserved, but it later reverted to *Empress*. (M.Turvey)